Contents

What is an atlas?   4

Hot and cold   6

About this atlas   8

World map   10

The Arctic and Antarctica   12

Canada   14

The United States   16

Central America and the Caribbean   18

South America   20

Northern Europe   22

Southern Europe   24

Russia and its neighbors   26

Southwest Asia   28

Northern Africa   30

Southern Africa   32

Southern Asia   34

Eastern Asia   36

Southeast Asia   38

Australia, New Zealand   40
   and the Pacific Islands

Fascinating facts   42

Index   44

What is an atlas?

An atlas is a book of maps showing different parts of the world. Maps are small pictures of big places drawn from above. They can show somewhere as small as a village or as big as the world. You can use atlases and maps in all sorts of ways. They might show you how to find your way around, or tell you what a place is like.

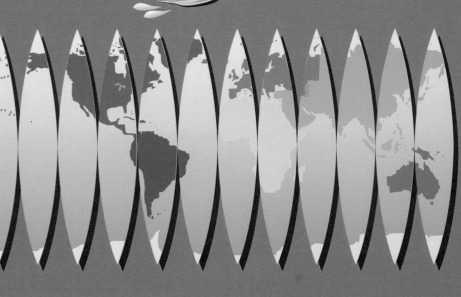

1 One of the most difficult maps to draw is one showing all of the world. This is because the world is round, like a huge ball, but maps are flat. Imagine painting the world onto the skin of an orange.

2 You could carefully peel the skin into segments.

3 Then you could lay the peel flat to make a map of the world.

4 Mapmakers fill the gaps by stretching some parts of the map and shrinking others.

On this map, you can see that more than half of the Earth is covered by four big oceans. The rest of the Earth is divided into seven huge areas of land, called continents. There are also three imaginary lines on the map. The equator circles the Earth's center. The Arctic Circle is at the top of the Earth and the Antarctic Circle is at the bottom.

ARCTIC OCEAN
Arctic Circle
NORTH AMERICA
EUROPE
ASIA
PACIFIC OCEAN
ATLANTIC OCEAN
AFRICA
Equator
SOUTH AMERICA
INDIAN OCEAN
AUSTRALIA
Antarctic Circle
ANTARCTICA

Different kinds of maps show different amounts of detail, but most maps show places much smaller than they really are.

1 This is a picture of a house on the corner of Park Street, which runs through a seaside town. You can see the hedge around the house, the tree outside and some of the street, but you cannot see the town or the sea because the picture is not big enough to show all these details.

2 This map shows Park Street from above. It shows less detail but a bigger area than before. Can you spot the house on the corner? Here, Park Street measures 4 inches (10cm), but it is really 1 mile (1km) long. This means that on the map every 4 inches (10cm) is the same as 1 mile (1km) in the real place. This is called *scale*.

Park Street

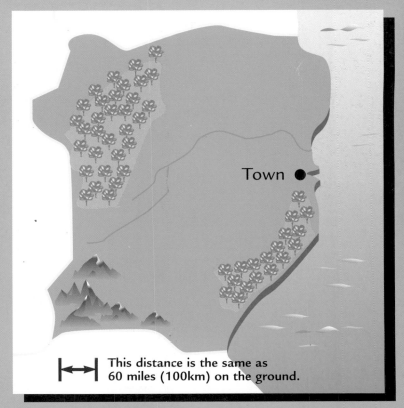

Town ●

This distance is the same as 60 miles (100km) on the ground.

3 This map shows a bigger area than the last map because it has a smaller scale. It shows all of the town. You cannot see the houses or all the streets, but you can see Park Street. On this map, Park Street is 2 inches (5cm) long. This means every 2 inches (5cm) on the map is the same as 1 mile (1km) in the real place.

4 This map shows the country where the town is found. The town is shown as a dot. The scale bar tells you that $3/_8$ inch (1cm) on the map is the same as 60 miles (100km) in the real place. In this atlas, each map has a different scale and scale bar. On pages 10-11 you can see all the whole world at the same scale.

Hot and cold

Around the world, there are different patterns of weather called climates. The climate of a country depends on where it is in the world. It is always hot near the equator and cold near the North and South Poles. On each map in this atlas, you will find a locator globe, showing you where countries and continents are in the world. The globe has arrows pointing to the four directions— north, south, east and west.

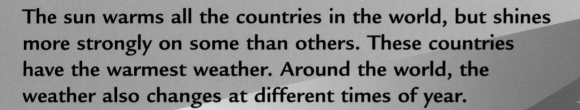

The sun warms all the countries in the world, but shines more strongly on some than others. These countries have the warmest weather. Around the world, the weather also changes at different times of year.

Arctic Circle

Around the North and South Poles, the sun is never high in the sky and shines weakly, so the land is always cold, especially in winter.

Tropic of Cancer

Near the equator, the sun shines strongest and directly from above. Here the climate is hot, with wet and dry seasons.

Equator

Tropic of Capricorn

Above and below the equator, there are two imaginary lines called the Tropic of Cancer and the Tropic of Capricorn. Countries between the tropics and the North and South Poles have warm summers and cold winters.

Different climates suit particular kinds of plants, and make different types of land for animals and people to live in. If a place has a rainy climate, lots of plants grow. If the climate is dry, fewer and different plants grow.

On the map below and the maps in this atlas, different types of land are shown by small pictures, called symbols, and colors. These photographs show you what the land really looks like.

Usually, the poles are icy cold. In summer, a few small plants grow around the Arctic.

Deciduous forests grow in cool areas. The trees lose their leaves in autumn.

Evergreen trees stay green all year. Evergreen forests grow in cold places.

Grassland includes tropical savanna (seen here), farmland and flat plains, called pampas.

Only the toughest plants and animals are able to survive in dry deserts.

Thick, green rainforests grow where it is warm and wet all year.

Few plants grow on rocky mountains, which are often covered in snow.

Arctic Circle

Tropic of Cancer

Equator

Tropic of Capricorn

This map shows different types of land found in the world.

Antarctic Circle

About this atlas

The maps in this atlas can tell you an enormous amount about the places they show. Look carefully at the pictures to find out more.

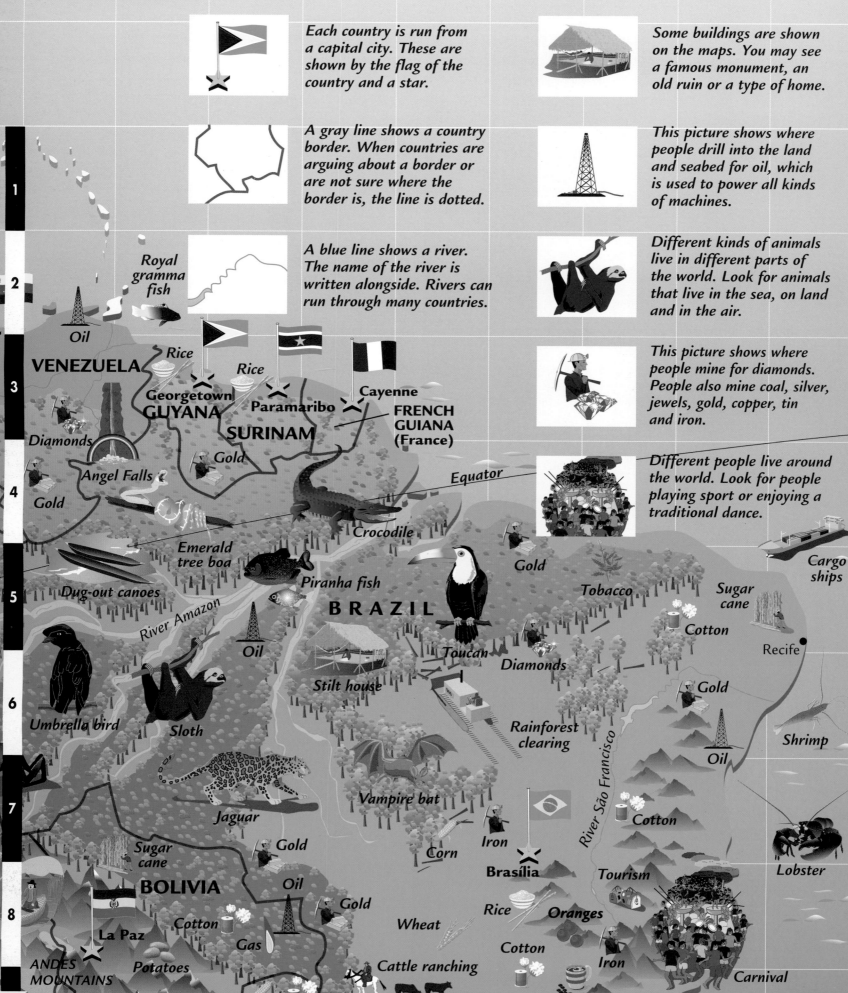

Crops grow all over the world. Look out for wheat, rice, fruit and vegetables. You may see coffee, tea and sugar cane, too.

Each country is run from a capital city. These are shown by the flag of the country and a star.

Some buildings are shown on the maps. You may see a famous monument, an old ruin or a type of home.

A gray line shows a country border. When countries are arguing about a border or are not sure where the border is, the line is dotted.

This picture shows where people drill into the land and seabed for oil, which is used to power all kinds of machines.

A blue line shows a river. The name of the river is written alongside. Rivers can run through many countries.

Different kinds of animals live in different parts of the world. Look for animals that live in the sea, on land and in the air.

This picture shows where people mine for diamonds. People also mine coal, silver, jewels, gold, copper, tin and iron.

Different people live around the world. Look for people playing sport or enjoying a traditional dance.

About the Factfile

Each map has a Factfile with facts about the places you can see. You might find out about a special animal or plant from a particular part of the world. Look at the picture beside each fact and then find it on the map. The facts in this Factfile are about the map of part of South America shown on the opposite page. Can you find all the pictures on the map?

On page 42, you will find a section of fascinating facts, full of many interesting things about the countries of the world.

Factfile

 South America is home to nearly one quarter of all known animals and around 2,500 different kinds of trees.

 The longest mountain range in the world is the Andes in South America.

Half of all the people in South America live in Brazil.

▼ This girl is answering the Fact Finder question. She is using a ruler and her finger to find the correct grid reference.

👉 FACT FINDER

Each map has a grid, which divides it into squares. The columns run up and down and have letters. The rows run from side to side and have numbers. This means each square has a name, or grid reference.

The Fact Finder asks questions about places on the map. You can find the answers by looking at the grid reference.

Here is a Fact Finder question about the map of part of South America shown on the opposite page.

► What is the name of the highest waterfall in the world? (See square E 4.)

To find square E 4, lay your ruler on column E, at the bottom of the map. Leave the ruler lying on the map. Now put your finger on row 4, at the side of the map. Run your finger along row 4 in a straight line. Square E 4 is where your finger meets the ruler.

You should have found Angel Falls which is in Venezuela.

World map

ARCTIC OCEAN

GREENLAND (Denmark)

ALASKA (USA)

CANADA

FINLAND   NORWAY

ICELAND

THE NETHERLANDS   SWEDEN

ESTONIA
LATVIA

UNITED KINGDOM

REPUBLIC OF IRELAND

BELGIUM

These countries in Europe are shown more clearly inside the circle on page 11.

FRANCE

UNITED STATES OF AMERICA

ATLANTIC OCEAN

ANDORRA

SPAIN

PORTUGAL

BALEARIC ISLANDS (Spain)

MALTA

AZORES (Portugal)

MADEIRA ISLANDS (Portugal)

MOROCCO

TUNISIA

CRETE (Greece)

BERMUDA (UK)

DOMINICAN REPUBLIC
PUERTO RICO (USA)
VIRGIN ISLANDS (USA & UK)
ANGUILLA (UK)
ST KITTS & NEVIS
ANTIGUA & BARBUDA
GUADELOUPE (France)
DOMINICA
MARTINIQUE (France)
ST LUCIA
BARBADOS
GRENADA
TRINIDAD & TOBAGO

MEXICO

BAHAMAS

CANARY ISLANDS (Spain)

ALGERIA

LIBYA

BELIZE

CUBA

WESTERN SAHARA

JAMAICA

GUATEMALA

HONDURAS   HAITI

CAPE VERDE ISLANDS

MAURITANIA

MALI

NIGER

CHAD

EL SALVADOR

NICARAGUA

MONTSERRAT (UK)

SENEGAL

ST VINCENT & THE GRENADINES

GAMBIA

BURKINA FASO

COSTA RICA

VENEZUELA

GUYANA

GUINEA-BISSAU

GUINEA

NIGERIA

CENTRAL AFRICAN REPUBLIC

PANAMA

SURINAM

SIERRA LEONE

IVORY COAST

GHANA

BENIN

TOGO

GALAPAGOS ISLANDS (Ecuador)

COLOMBIA

FRENCH GUIANA (France)

LIBERIA

CAMEROON

ECUADOR

SÃO TOMÉ & PRÍNCIPE

GABON

ZAIRE

EQUATORIAL GUINEA

CONGO

PERU

BRAZIL

CABINDA (Angola)

ANGOLA

PACIFIC OCEAN

ZAMBIA

BOLIVIA

NAMIBIA

PARAGUAY

BOTSWANA

The world is divided into almost 200 countries and this map shows most of them. The countries are different colors so that you can tell them apart. Some countries own places in other parts of the world. In this atlas, these kinds of places have two labels. One label gives their name and another label in brackets gives the name of the country that owns them.

CHILE

URUGUAY

ATLANTIC OCEAN

REPUBLIC OF SOUTH AFRICA

ARGENTINA

LESOTHO

FALKLAND ISLANDS (UK)

SOUTH GEORGIA (UK)

ANTARCTICA

RUSSIA

KAZAKHSTAN

UKRAINE

AZERBAIJAN

ARMENIA

GEORGIA

TURKEY

CYPRUS

SYRIA

LEBANON

IRAQ

JORDAN

ISRAEL

EGYPT

SUDAN

ERITREA

DJIBOUTI

ETHIOPIA

UGANDA

KENYA

RWANDA

BURUNDI

TANZANIA

MALAWI

COMOROS

MAYOTTE (France)

MADAGASCAR

ZIMBABWE

MOZAMBIQUE

SWAZILAND

UZBEKISTAN

TURKMENISTAN

KYRGYZSTAN

TAJIKISTAN

AFGHANISTAN

IRAN

KUWAIT

BAHRAIN

QATAR

UNITED ARAB EMIRATES

SAUDI ARABIA

OMAN

YEMEN

SOCOTRA (Yemen)

SOMALIA

SEYCHELLES

PAKISTAN

NEPAL

BHUTAN

INDIA

BANGLADESH

MALDIVE ISLANDS

SRI LANKA

ANDAMAN ISLANDS (India)

NICOBAR ISLANDS (India)

MONGOLIA

CHINA

MYANMAR

MACAO (Portugal)

LAOS

THAILAND

CAMBODIA

VIETNAM

HONG KONG (UK)

NORTH KOREA

SOUTH KOREA

JAPAN

TAIWAN (China)

PHILIPPINES

BRUNEI

MALAYSIA

SINGAPORE

INDONESIA

IRIAN JAYA (Indonesia)

PACIFIC OCEAN

NORTHERN MARIANAS (USA)

GUAM (USA)

MARSHALL ISLANDS

PALAU (USA)

STATES OF MICRONESIA

NAURU

KIRIBATI

PAPUA NEW GUINEA

SOLOMON ISLANDS

TUVALU

INDIAN OCEAN

AUSTRALIA

TASMANIA (Australia)

VANUATU

FIJI

NEW CALEDONIA (France)

NEW ZEALAND

SWEDEN

LATVIA

LITHUANIA

(Russia)

DENMARK

BELARUS

GERMANY

POLAND

LUXEMBOURG

CZECH REPUBLIC

SLOVAKIA

UKRAINE

LIECHTENSTEIN

AUSTRIA

HUNGARY

MOLDOVA

SWITZERLAND

SLOVENIA

CROATIA

ROMANIA

SAN MARINO

FEDERAL REPUBLIC OF YUGOSLAVIA

MONACO

BOSNIA-HERZEGOVINA

BULGARIA

CORSICA (France)

ITALY

MACEDONIA

TURKEY

SARDINIA (Italy)

ALBANIA

VATICAN CITY

GREECE

SICILY (Italy)

Some countries in Europe are crowded together. In this circle, we have made these countries bigger so that you can see them more easily.

The Arctic

The Arctic is the part of the world that lies closest to the North Pole. Around the Pole, the Arctic Ocean is frozen all year, but further away the ice and snow melt in the summer. In winter, the sun hardly shines, which makes the Arctic very cold. Very little grows there, except for a few small plants such as moss or lichen.

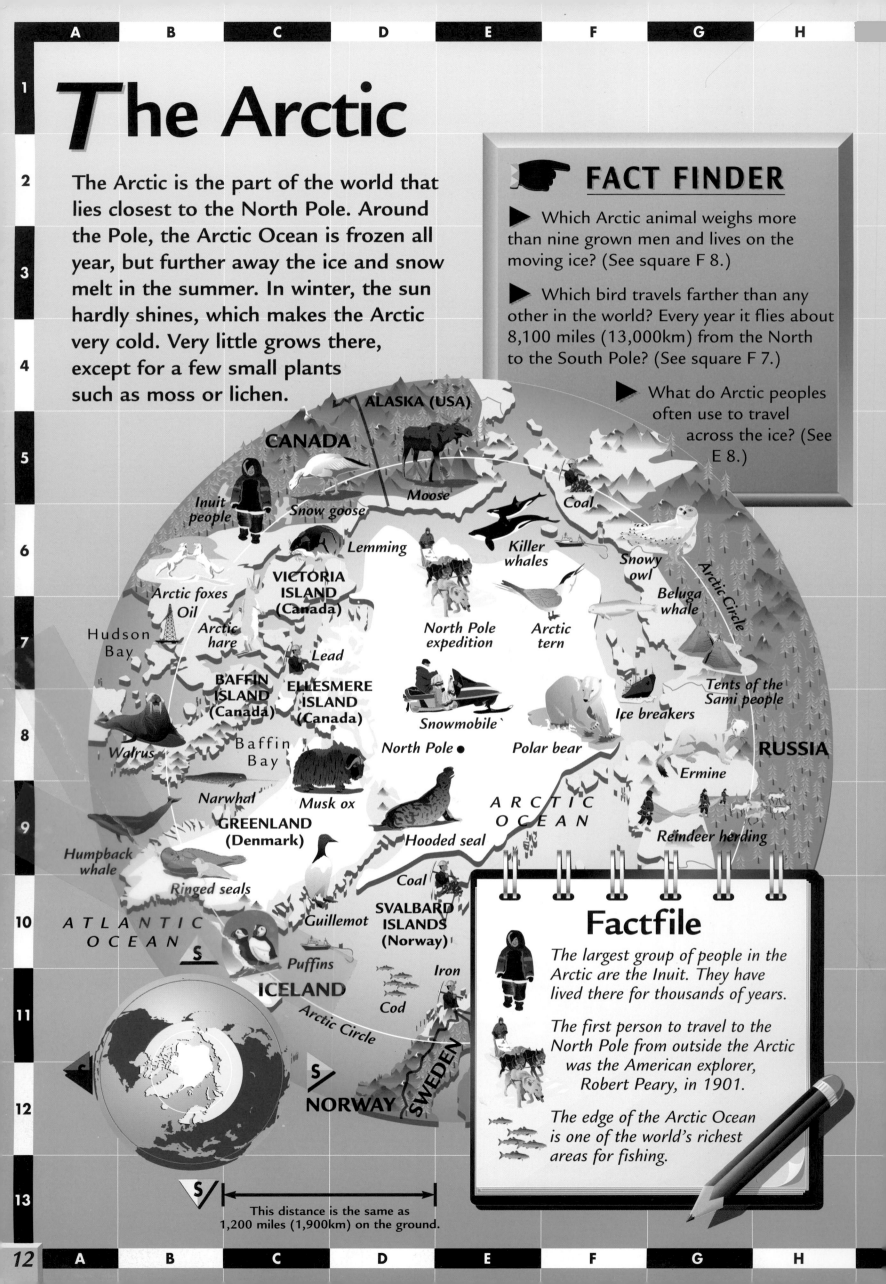

ALASKA (USA)

CANADA

Inuit people

Snow goose

Moose

Coal

Lemming

Killer whales

Snowy owl

Arctic Circle

VICTORIA ISLAND (Canada)

Arctic foxes

Oil

Beluga whale

Hudson Bay

Arctic hare

North Pole expedition

Arctic tern

Lead

Tents of the Sami people

BAFFIN ISLAND (Canada)

ELLESMERE ISLAND (Canada)

Snowmobile

Ice breakers

Walrus

Baffin Bay

North Pole ●

Polar bear

RUSSIA

Ermine

Narwhal

Musk ox

A R C T I C   O C E A N

GREENLAND (Denmark)

Hooded seal

Reindeer herding

Humpback whale

Ringed seals

Coal

Guillemot

SVALBARD ISLANDS (Norway)

A T L A N T I C   O C E A N

S

Puffins

Iron

ICELAND

Cod

Arctic Circle

S

S

NORWAY

SWEDEN

This distance is the same as 1,200 miles (1,900km) on the ground.

Factfile

The largest group of people in the Arctic are the Inuit. They have lived there for thousands of years.

The first person to travel to the North Pole from outside the Arctic was the American explorer, Robert Peary, in 1901.

The edge of the Arctic Ocean is one of the world's richest areas for fishing.

Antarctica

Antarctica is an enormous ice-covered continent near the South Pole. It is the coldest and windiest place on Earth. Few animals live around the pole but there are seals and birds on the coast, and plants and fish in the sea. The only people living in Antarctica are scientists. They stay on research stations to study the land and its wildlife.

Factfile

In 1911, Roald Amundsen, a Norwegian explorer, became the first person to reach the South Pole.

Up to 30,000 tourists a year cruise the waters around Antarctica to see the land and its wildlife.

Antarctica has many icebergs. The largest one ever found was over twice the size of the state of Delaware.

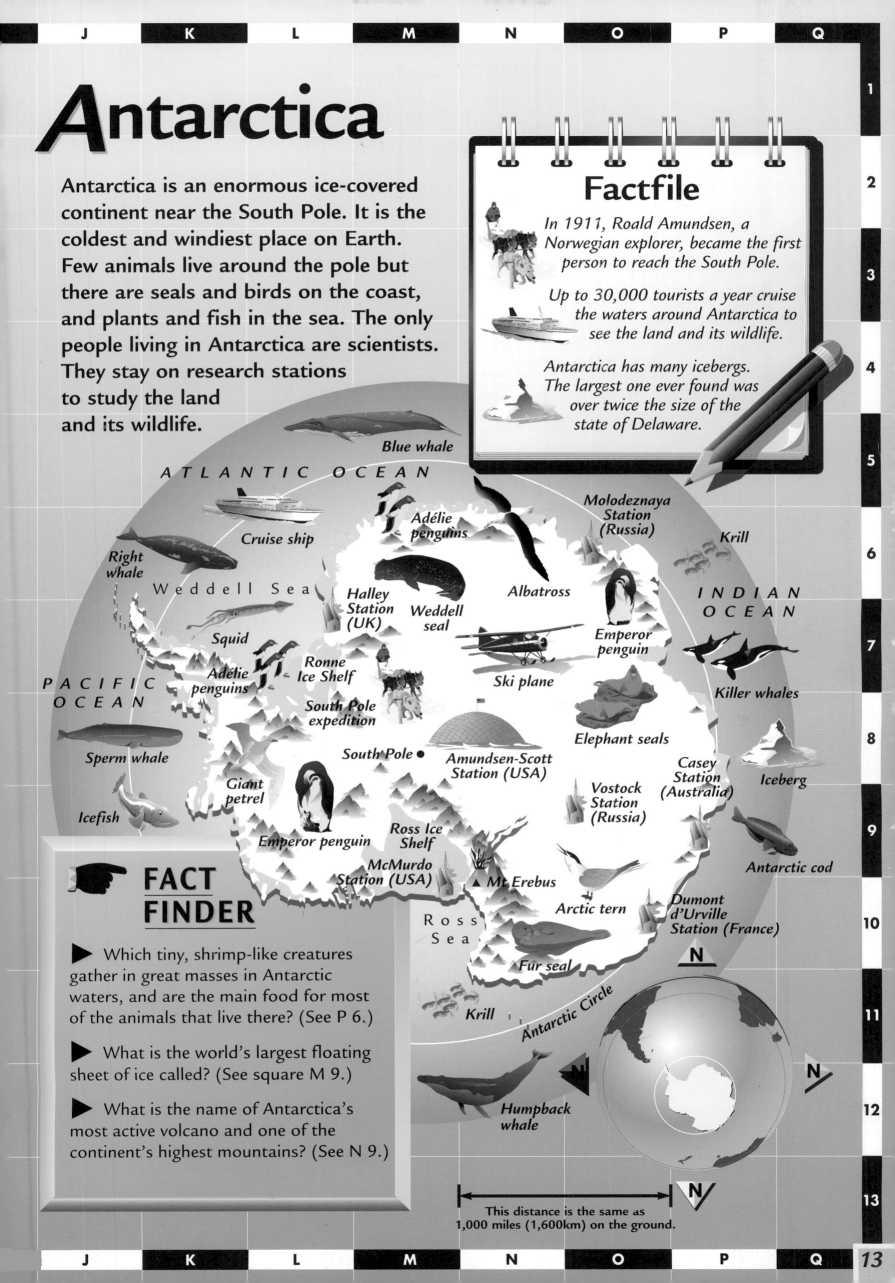

Blue whale

ATLANTIC OCEAN

Cruise ship

Adélie penguins

Molodeznaya Station (Russia)

Krill

Right whale

Weddell Sea

Halley Station (UK)

Weddell seal

Albatross

INDIAN OCEAN

Squid

Adélie penguins

Ronne Ice Shelf

Emperor penguin

PACIFIC OCEAN

South Pole expedition

Ski plane

Killer whales

Sperm whale

South Pole ●

Amundsen-Scott Station (USA)

Elephant seals

Casey Station (Australia)

Iceberg

Giant petrel

Vostock Station (Russia)

Icefish

Emperor penguin

Ross Ice Shelf

McMurdo Station (USA)

▲ Mt Erebus

Antarctic cod

Arctic tern

Dumont d'Urville Station (France)

Ross Sea

Fur seal

N

Antarctic Circle

Krill

Humpback whale

FACT FINDER

▶ Which tiny, shrimp-like creatures gather in great masses in Antarctic waters, and are the main food for most of the animals that live there? (See P 6.)

▶ What is the world's largest floating sheet of ice called? (See square M 9.)

▶ What is the name of Antarctica's most active volcano and one of the continent's highest mountains? (See N 9.)

N

N

N

This distance is the same as 1,000 miles (1,600km) on the ground.

Canada

Canada is the second biggest country in the world after Russia. Large parts of it are cold and empty. In the north, there are huge pine forests and the weather is often freezing. Most people live in the south where it is warmer. Canada produces oil and mines coal, silver, gold and copper. It has good farmland, where farmers grow enormous fields of wheat. It also has large factories, mostly in the east, that make and sell goods, such as cars, trucks and trains.

ARCTIC OCEAN

Arctic tern

Ice breakers

Parry Islands

Killer whales

Banks Island

Canadian Royal Mounted Police

Musk ox

Victoria Island

ALASKA

Salmon

YUKON TERRITORY

Oil

Husky dogs

Mt Logan

Great Bear Lake

Tourism

Silver

River Yukon

River Mackenzie

Arctic foxes

NORTHWEST

Silver

Wolf

Gold

Arctic hare

Mountain goat

Gas

Great Slave Lake

Oil

Indian carvings

N

W

E

S

Bald eagle

Brown bear

Black bear

ALBERTA

Tourism

PACIFIC OCEAN

Herring

Gas

Ice hockey

Forestry

Forestry

Grizzly bear

Coal

SASKATCHEWAN

BRITISH COLUMBIA

Edmonton

Apples

Oil

Vancouver

Wheat

Buffalo

Barley

Oil

Wheat

Skiing

Pronghorn antelope

Wheat

FACT FINDER

► Which game is played using a puck and stick on a large ice rink, and is the country's most popular sport? (See square F 9.)

► Which large animal once roamed in huge herds over Canada's grasslands but now lives mostly in national parks? (See square H 10.)

► Canada has two main languages, English and French. In which province, or district, would you find most of the French speakers? (See square N 9.)

UNITED STATES OF AMERICA

This distance is the same as 500 miles (800km) on the ground.

14

J K L M N O P Q
1 2 3 4 5 6 7 8 9 10 11 12 13

GREENLAND (Denmark)

Ellesmere Island

Queen Elizabeth Islands

Lemming

Walrus

Beluga whale

Hooded seal

Narwhal

Prince of Wales Island

Inuit people

Baffin Island

Snowy owl

Snowmobile

Arctic Circle

Polar bear

T E R R I T O R I E S

Starfish

Humpback whale

A T L A N T I C O C E A N

Factfile

Forests cover more than one-third of Canada. The trees are cut down by lumberjacks and made into timber and paper.

Canada is famous for its sweet maple syrup. It is made in the spring from the sticky sap of sugar maple trees.

In Canada no one is far from water. The country has over one million lakes. Lake Superior, on the border between Canada and the United States, is the largest freshwater lake in the world.

Canada geese

Ice breakers

Lynx

Iron

Puffins

Right whale

H u d s o n B a y

Mink

Snow goose

Float plane

NEWFOUNDLAND

Cod

Moose

MANITOBA

River Nelson

Beaver

Ermine

QUEBEC

Forestry

Maple syrup

Iron

Forestry

Making paper

Copper

Tourism

ONTARIO

Red squirrel

Gold

Tourist bus

Copper

G u l f o f St Lawrence

Oil

Road train

Château Frontenac

Dairy cattle

Winnipeg

Racoon

Iron

River St Lawrence

NEW BRUNSWICK

NOVA SCOTIA

Beef cattle

Iron

Lake Superior

CN Tower

Potatoes

Apples

Montreal

Ottawa

Coal

Lake Huron

Car building

PRINCE EDWARD ISLAND

Blue whale

Toronto

Lake Ontario

Lake Michigan

Pigs

Lake Erie

Niagara Falls

Lobster

The United States

Tuna

Building airliners

Corn

Seattle

WASHINGTON

Oil

Apples

Black bear

Raccoon

Right whale

Arctic Circle

Volcanoes

MONTANA

Polar bear

Forestry

Grizzly bear

Old Faithful Geyser

ALASKA

OREGON

IDAHO

Coal

Yukon River

Oil pipeline

Mt McKinley

Pronghorn antelope

Wild horses

Beef cattle

WYOMING

Fur seals

Bald eagle

Buffalo

Beef cattle

Husky dogs

Anchorage

Gold

Great Salt Lake

Rocky Mountain goat

Forestry

Oranges

Silver

Golden Gate Bridge

Beef cattle

Copper

COLORADO

Denve

Wild horses

NEVADA

Wild horses

UTAH

Salmon

San Francisco

Skiing

San Jose

Humpback whale

Gulf of Alaska

Computer chip

Wine

CALIFORNIA

Tourism

HOLLYWOOD

Oil

Gas

NEW MEXICO

The United States is a huge land made up of fifty areas, called states, including Alaska and Hawaii. It has many different peoples and landscapes. In the west there are high mountains, forests and spectacular scenery. In the middle is a huge plain which is perfect for growing wheat and corn. The northeast has smaller mountains, coal mines and car factories. Here there are cities, such as New York, with tall skyscrapers. Over the last five hundred years, millions of people have moved to the United States to live.

Making films

Los Angeles

Grand Canyon

Phoenix

San Diego

Oil

Sea lion

Saguaro cactus

ARIZONA

Sidewinder snake

El Paso

Rio Gra

MEXICO

Surfing

PACIFIC OCEAN

HAWAII

Octopus

Volcanoes

Tourism

Factfile

The Bald eagle is the national bird of the United States. It is found mainly in the state of Alaska, where there are lots of fish, its favorite food.

Nearly half of the world's corn is grown in the United States.

The US flag has a star for every state in the United States of America.

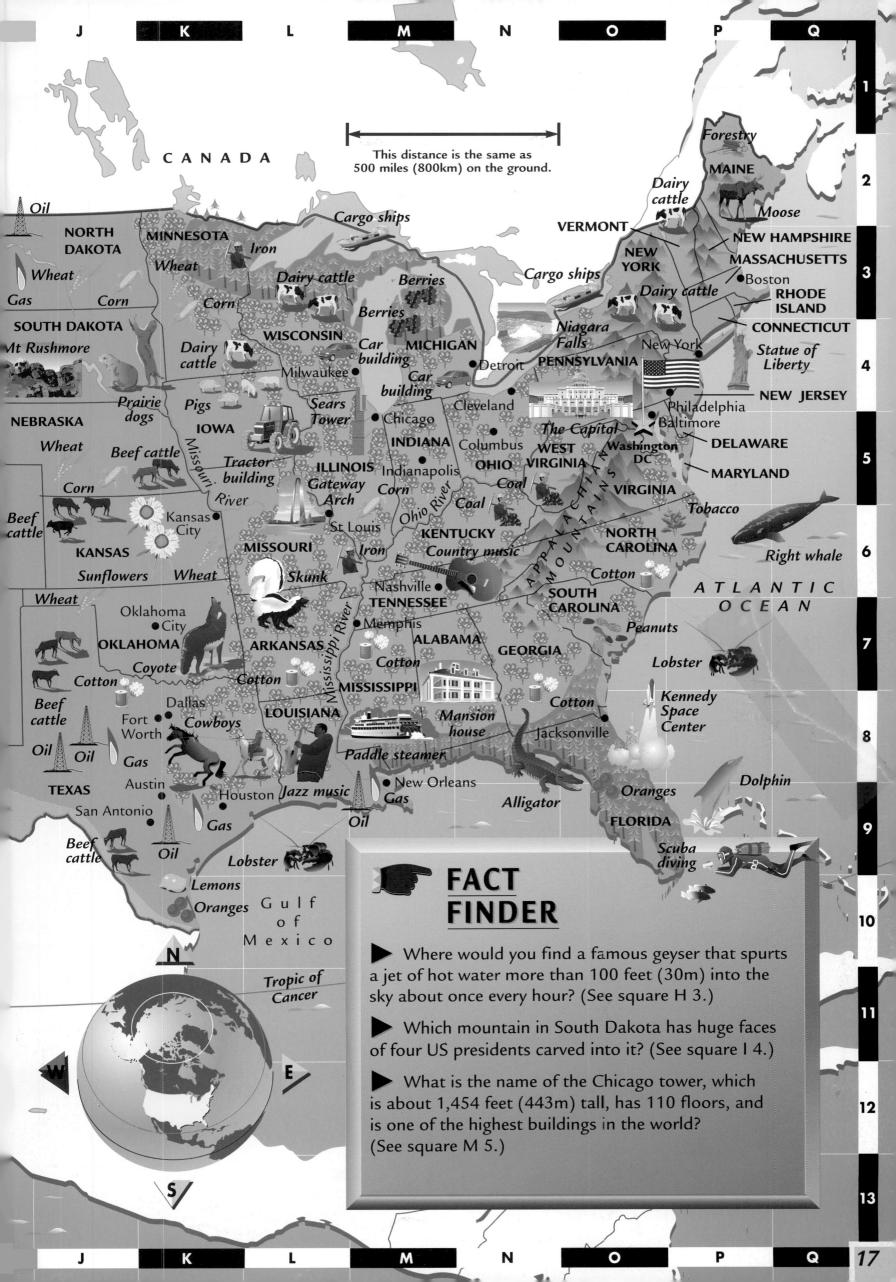

CANADA

This distance is the same as 500 miles (800km) on the ground.

Oil

NORTH DAKOTA

MINNESOTA

Iron

Cargo ships

Forestry

MAINE

Moose

Dairy cattle

VERMONT

NEW HAMPSHIRE

MASSACHUSETTS

Wheat

Wheat

Dairy cattle

Berries

NEW YORK

Boston

RHODE ISLAND

Gas

Corn

Corn

WISCONSIN

Berries

MICHIGAN

Cargo ships

Dairy cattle

CONNECTICUT

SOUTH DAKOTA

Dairy cattle

Car building

Niagara Falls

New York

PENNSYLVANIA

Statue of Liberty

Mt Rushmore

Milwaukee

Car building

Detroit

Cleveland

NEW JERSEY

Prairie dogs

Pigs

Sears Tower

Chicago

The Capital

Philadelphia

Baltimore

DELAWARE

NEBRASKA

IOWA

INDIANA

Columbus

WEST VIRGINIA

Washington DC

MARYLAND

Wheat

Beef cattle

Tractor building

ILLINOIS

Indianapolis

OHIO

Coal

VIRGINIA

Corn

Gateway Arch

Corn

Coal

Tobacco

Beef cattle

Kansas City

St Louis

KENTUCKY

Country music

NORTH CAROLINA

Right whale

KANSAS

MISSOURI

Iron

Skunk

Nashville

SOUTH CAROLINA

Cotton

ATLANTIC OCEAN

Sunflowers

Wheat

TENNESSEE

Memphis

ALABAMA

GEORGIA

Peanuts

Wheat

Oklahoma City

Coyote

ARKANSAS

Cotton

Cotton

Lobster

OKLAHOMA

Mansion house

Kennedy Space Center

Cotton

Cotton

MISSISSIPPI

Beef cattle

Dallas

Cowboys

LOUISIANA

Jacksonville

Oranges

Dolphin

Oil

Oil

Gas

Fort Worth

Paddle steamer

Oil

New Orleans

Jazz music

Gas

Alligator

FLORIDA

TEXAS

Austin

Houston

San Antonio

Gas

Beef cattle

Oil

Lobster

Scuba diving

Lemons

Oranges

Gulf of Mexico

N

W

E

S

Tropic of Cancer

FACT FINDER

▶ Where would you find a famous geyser that spurts a jet of hot water more than 100 feet (30m) into the sky about once every hour? (See square H 3.)

▶ Which mountain in South Dakota has huge faces of four US presidents carved into it? (See square I 4.)

▶ What is the name of the Chicago tower, which is about 1,454 feet (443m) tall, has 110 floors, and is one of the highest buildings in the world? (See square M 5.)

Central America and the Caribbean

A B C D E F G H

UNITED STATES
OF AMERICA

N
W
E
S

Saguaro cactus

BAJA CALIFORNIA

Beef cattle

Cotton

Silver

Sea lion

Rio Grande

Armadillo

Rice

Coyote

Beef cattle

Cotton

SIERRA MADRE

MEXICO

Elephant seals

Gulf of Mexico

Blue whale

Grapefruit

Lobster

PACIFIC
OCEAN

Spectacled bear

Lemons

Anchovies

Tobacco

Oranges

Tourism

Corn

Humpback whale

Corn

Shrimp

Chichén Itzá

Tourism

Forestry

Oil

Iron

Mexico City

Scarlet macaw

Spider monkey

Polka dot grouper fish

Tourism

Sugar cane

• Acapulco

Corn

Corn

Belmopan

BELIZE

Coffee

Factfile

Mexico is one of the world's biggest producers of silver.

The Caribbean Islands are some of the world's most popular holiday places. Cruise ships carry passengers from one island to another.

Honduras is one of the world's largest producers of bananas. The fruit is green when it is picked, but ripens as it is shipped across the world.

Teardrop butterfly fish

GUATEMALA

Guatemala City

San Salvador

Tegucig alp

EL SALVADOR

Coffee

Managua

Swordfish

Clown fish

This distance is the same as 430 miles (700km) on the ground.

Sea horses

Sperm whale

A B C D E F G H

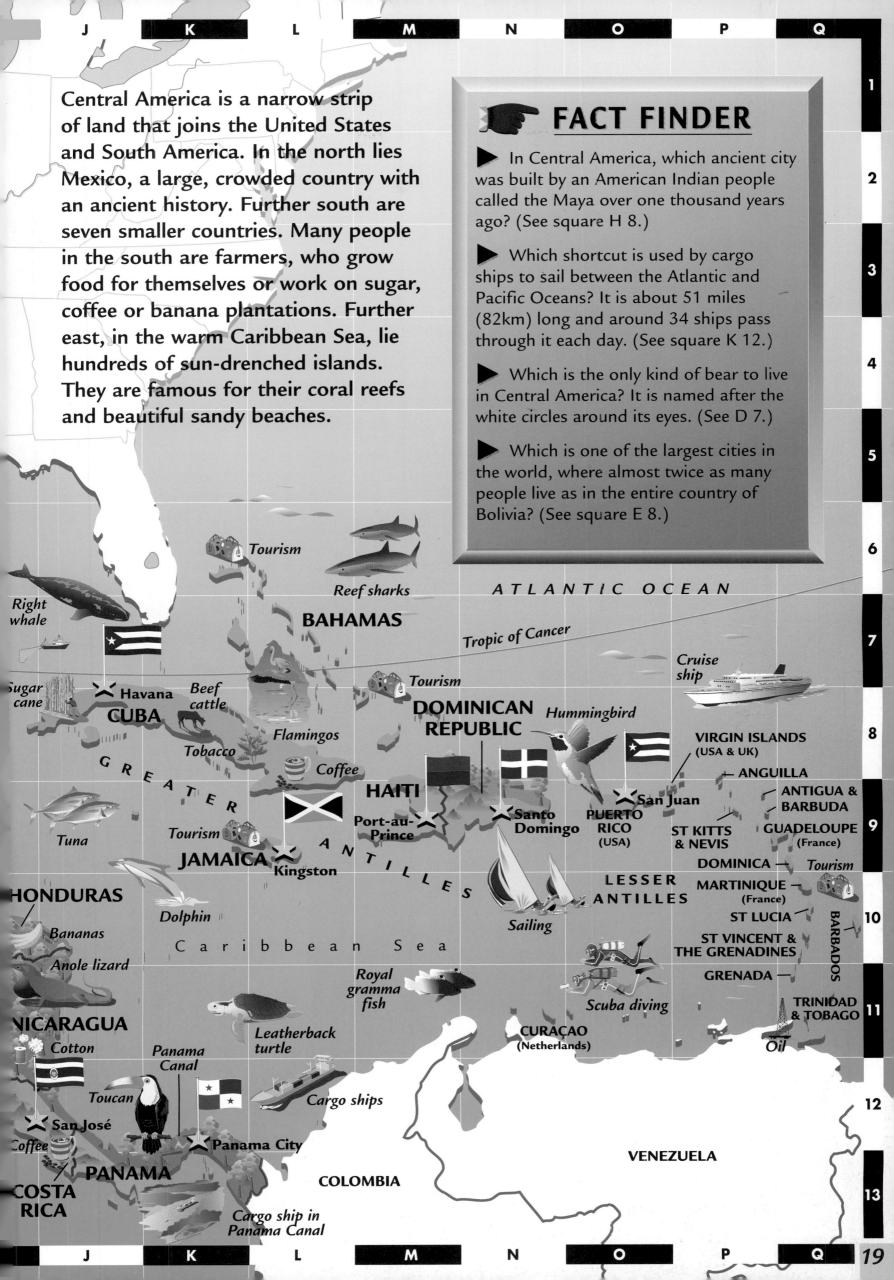

Central America is a narrow strip of land that joins the United States and South America. In the north lies Mexico, a large, crowded country with an ancient history. Further south are seven smaller countries. Many people in the south are farmers, who grow food for themselves or work on sugar, coffee or banana plantations. Further east, in the warm Caribbean Sea, lie hundreds of sun-drenched islands. They are famous for their coral reefs and beautiful sandy beaches.

FACT FINDER

▶ In Central America, which ancient city was built by an American Indian people called the Maya over one thousand years ago? (See square H 8.)

▶ Which shortcut is used by cargo ships to sail between the Atlantic and Pacific Oceans? It is about 51 miles (82km) long and around 34 ships pass through it each day. (See square K 12.)

▶ Which is the only kind of bear to live in Central America? It is named after the white circles around its eyes. (See D 7.)

▶ Which is one of the largest cities in the world, where almost twice as many people live as in the entire country of Bolivia? (See square E 8.)

Tourism

Reef sharks

ATLANTIC OCEAN

Right whale

BAHAMAS

Tropic of Cancer

Cruise ship

Sugar cane

Havana

Beef cattle

CUBA

Tourism

DOMINICAN REPUBLIC

Hummingbird

VIRGIN ISLANDS (USA & UK)

Flamingos

Tobacco

Coffee

← ANGUILLA

G R E A T E R

HAITI

San Juan

ANTIGUA & BARBUDA

Tuna

Tourism

Port-au-Prince

Santo Domingo

PUERTO RICO (USA)

ST KITTS & NEVIS

GUADELOUPE (France)

JAMAICA

Kingston

A N T I L L E S

DOMINICA →

Tourism

HONDURAS

LESSER ANTILLES

MARTINIQUE — (France)

Dolphin

ST LUCIA →

BARBADOS

Bananas

Sailing

ST VINCENT & THE GRENADINES

Anole lizard

C a r i b b e a n   S e a

GRENADA —

Royal gramma fish

Scuba diving

TRINIDAD & TOBAGO

NICARAGUA

Leatherback turtle

CURAÇAO (Netherlands)

Oil

Cotton

Panama Canal

Toucan

Cargo ships

San José

Coffee

Panama City

VENEZUELA

PANAMA

COLOMBIA

COSTA RICA

Cargo ship in Panama Canal

1
2
3
4
5
6
7
8
9
10
11
12
13

South America

The continent of South America stretches from the warm Caribbean Sea to the stormy waters around Cape Horn. South America is warm all year, except in the far south and in the high Andes Mountains.

In the north, the great River Amazon flows through tropical rainforest. Further south, there are flat plains where millions of cattle graze. Most South Americans live in cities on the coast. In the country, the farmers grow bananas, coffee beans and corn.

Caribbean Sea

Cargo ships

Tourism
Bananas
Gold

Royal gramma fish
Rice
Oil
Oil
Oil
Oil

Caracas Oil
VENEZUELA
Bogotá
Coffee
COLOMBIA
Cow tree
Making clothes
River Orinoco
Diamonds
Gold
Stilt house
Emeralds
Cali
Quito
ECUADOR
Oil
Coffee
Bananas
Herring
Coffee

Cayenne
FRENCH GUIANA (France)
Paramaribo
SURINAME
Rice
Georgetown
GUYANA
Gold
Angel Falls
Emerald tree boa
Crocodile
Piranha fish
Oil
Dug-out canoes
River Amazon
Shrimp
Equator
Toucan
Amazon rainforest
Vampire bat
Sloth
Jaguar
Umbrella bird
Arrow-poison frog
Tapir
Coffee
Copper
PERU
Lima
Gold
Lake Titicaca
Llama
Cotton
Sugar cane
Sperm whale

Cargo ships
Shrimp
Lobster
Recife
Sugar cane
Cotton
Gold
Oil
Cotton
River São Francisco
Tourism
Carnival
Rio de Janeiro
Coffee
Cotton
Iron
Oranges
Rice
Brasília
Iron
Corn
Gold
BRAZIL
Rainforest clearing
Diamonds
Gold
Tobacco

Oil
Gold
Gas
Cotton
Corn
BOLIVIA
La Paz
Cotton
Potatoes
Copper
Wheat
Cattle ranching
Gold
Sugar cane

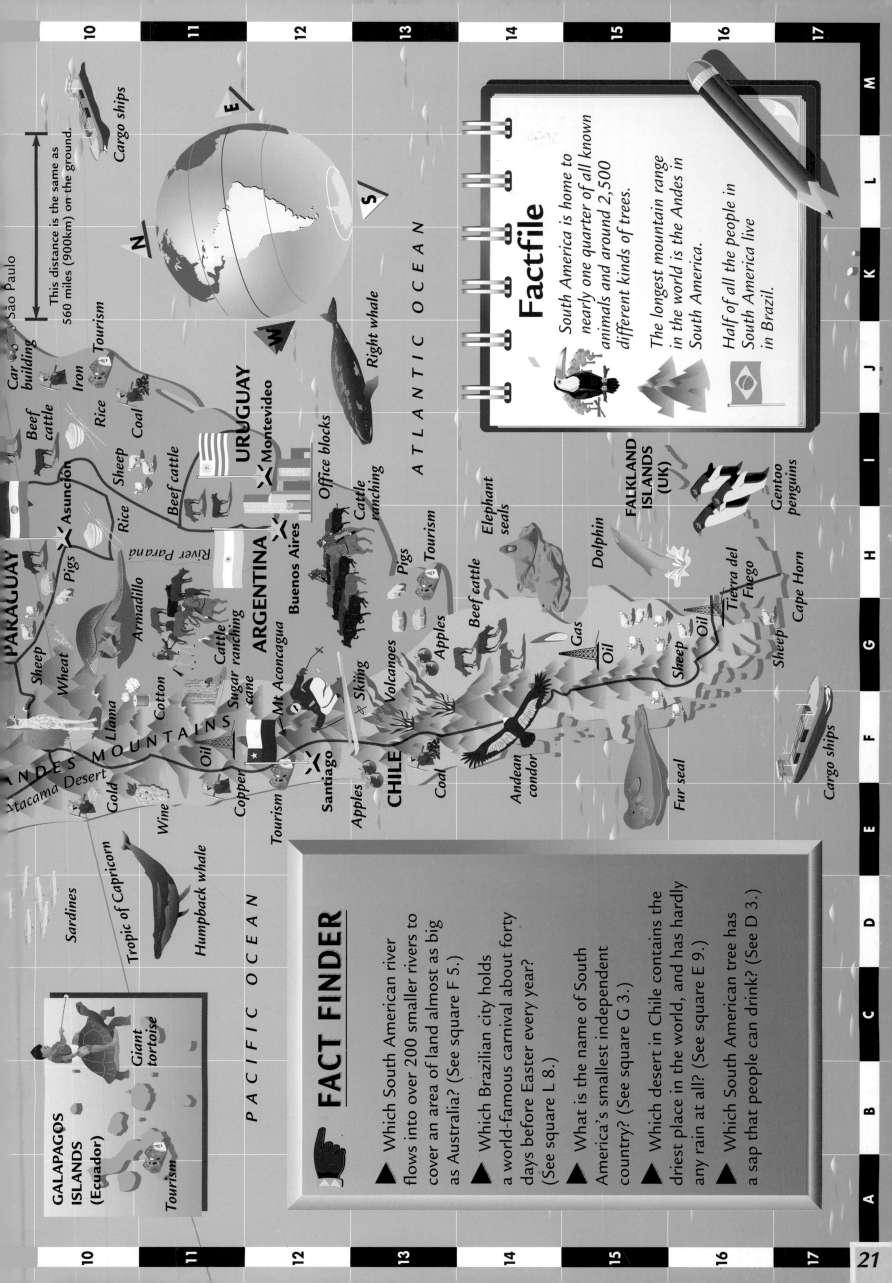

GALAPAGOS ISLANDS (Ecuador)

Giant tortoise

Tourism

Sardines

Tropic of Capricorn

Humpback whale

PACIFIC OCEAN

Cargo ships

This distance is the same as 560 miles (900km) on the ground.

Car go o São Paulo building

Iron

Tourism

Beef cattle

Rice

Coal

Sheep

Rice

Beef cattle

PARAGUAY

Asunción

Pigs

Sheep

Wheat

Llama

Armadillo

Cotton

Sugar cane

Cattle ranching

River Paraná

URUGUAY

Montevideo

Office blocks

ARGENTINA

Buenos Aires

Cattle ranching

Pigs

Tourism

Apples

Right whale

ATLANTIC OCEAN

ANDES MOUNTAINS

Atacama Desert

Gold

Wine

Oil

Copper

Tourism

Santiago

Apples

CHILE

Coal

Volcanoes

Skiing

Mt Aconcagua

Andean condor

Beef cattle

Elephant seals

Gas

Oil

Dolphin

FALKLAND ISLANDS (UK)

Gentoo penguins

Sheep

Oil

Tierra del Fuego

Cape Horn

Sheep

Fur seal

Cargo ships

N E S W

Factfile

South America is home to nearly one quarter of all known animals and around 2,500 different kinds of trees.

The longest mountain range in the world is the Andes in South America.

Half of all the people in South America live in Brazil.

FACT FINDER

▲ Which South American river flows into over 200 smaller rivers to cover an area of land almost as big as Australia? (See square F 5.)

▲ Which Brazilian city holds a world-famous carnival about forty days before Easter every year? (See square L 8.)

▲ What is the name of South America's smallest independent country? (See square G 3.)

▲ Which desert in Chile contains the driest place in the world, and has hardly any rain at all? (See square E 9.)

▲ Which South American tree has a sap that people can drink? (See D 3.)

Northern Europe

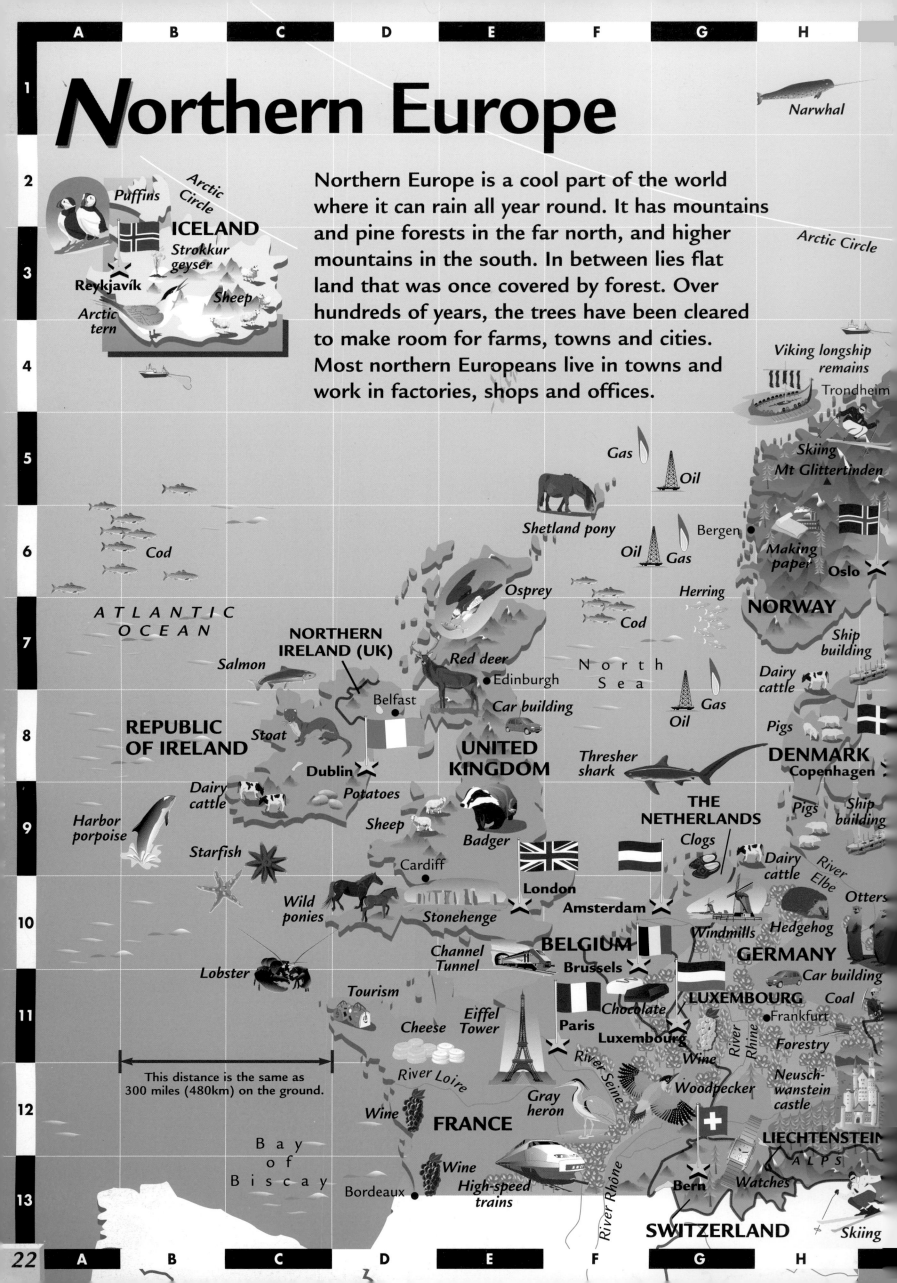

Narwhal

Northern Europe is a cool part of the world where it can rain all year round. It has mountains and pine forests in the far north, and higher mountains in the south. In between lies flat land that was once covered by forest. Over hundreds of years, the trees have been cleared to make room for farms, towns and cities. Most northern Europeans live in towns and work in factories, shops and offices.

Arctic Circle

Puffins
Arctic Circle
ICELAND
Strokkur geyser
Reykjavík
Sheep
Arctic tern

Viking longship remains
Trondheim

Skiing
Mt Glittertinden

Gas
Oil
Shetland pony
Bergen
Oil
Gas
Making paper
Oslo
NORWAY
Herring
Osprey
Cod
Ship building

ATLANTIC OCEAN

Cod

NORTHERN IRELAND (UK)

Salmon

Red deer
Edinburgh
North Sea
Dairy cattle

REPUBLIC OF IRELAND
Stoat
Belfast
Car building
UNITED KINGDOM
Oil
Gas
Pigs
DENMARK
Copenhagen

Dublin
Dairy cattle
Potatoes
Thresher shark
THE NETHERLANDS
Pigs
Ship building

Harbor porpoise
Sheep
Badger
Clogs
Dairy cattle
River Elbe
Otters

Starfish
Cardiff
London
Amsterdam
Windmills
Hedgehog

Wild ponies
Stonehenge
BELGIUM
Brussels
GERMANY
Car building

Lobster
Channel Tunnel
Chocolate
LUXEMBOURG
Coal

Tourism
Eiffel Tower
Paris
Luxembourg
Frankfurt

Cheese
Wine
Forestry

This distance is the same as 300 miles (480km) on the ground.

River Loire
Gray heron
Woodpecker
Wine
Neuschwanstein castle

Wine
FRANCE
River Seine
River Rhine

Bay of Biscay
Wine
High-speed trains
Bern
Watches
LIECHTENSTEIN
ALPS

Bordeaux
River Rhône
SWITZERLAND
Skiing

Map labels

Norwegian Sea

KJØLEN MOUNTAINS

Lapland
Reindeer
Sami people
Iron
Forestry
Cross-country skiing
Forestry
Forestry
Making paper
SWEDEN
Salmon
Herring
Fox
Stockholm
Ice breakers
Car building
Göteborg
Dairy cattle
Ship building
Ship building
Malmö
Baltic Sea

FINLAND
Lynx
Making paper
Helsinki

Tallinn
Pigs
ESTONIA
Building trains
Riga
LATVIA
LITHUANIA
Vilnius
Kaliningrad (Russia)
Dairy cattle

RUSSIA
BELARUS

Potatoes
Red squirrel
Wild boar
Berlin
Warsaw
Chaffinch
POLAND
Coal
Wolf
Chamois
UKRAINE

Prague
CZECH REPUBLIC
SLOVAKIA
Vienna
River Danube
Bratislava
AUSTRIA
Peregrine falcon
Budapest
Parliament building
HUNGARY
Wild horses
ROMANIA

N W E S

FACT FINDER

▶ Which tunnel in northern Europe is about 31 miles (50km) long, was opened in 1994 and is often called the "Chunnel"? (See square E 10.)

▶ In which country could you see a long ship on display, which was built by the Viking people hundreds of years ago? (See square H 4.)

▶ Which famous European tower is about 984 feet (320m) high and has 1,652 steps that take you to the top? (See square E 11.)

▶ Which stone monument in England was built around 3,500 years ago, but nobody knows what it was used for? (See square E 10.)

Factfile

There are twice as many pigs in Denmark as people. Two out of three pigs are exported as Danish bacon.

France is visited by more tourists each year than any other country in the world.

Finland produces enough paper to make 5 million comics every day.

1 2 3 4 5 6 7 8 9 10 11 12 13

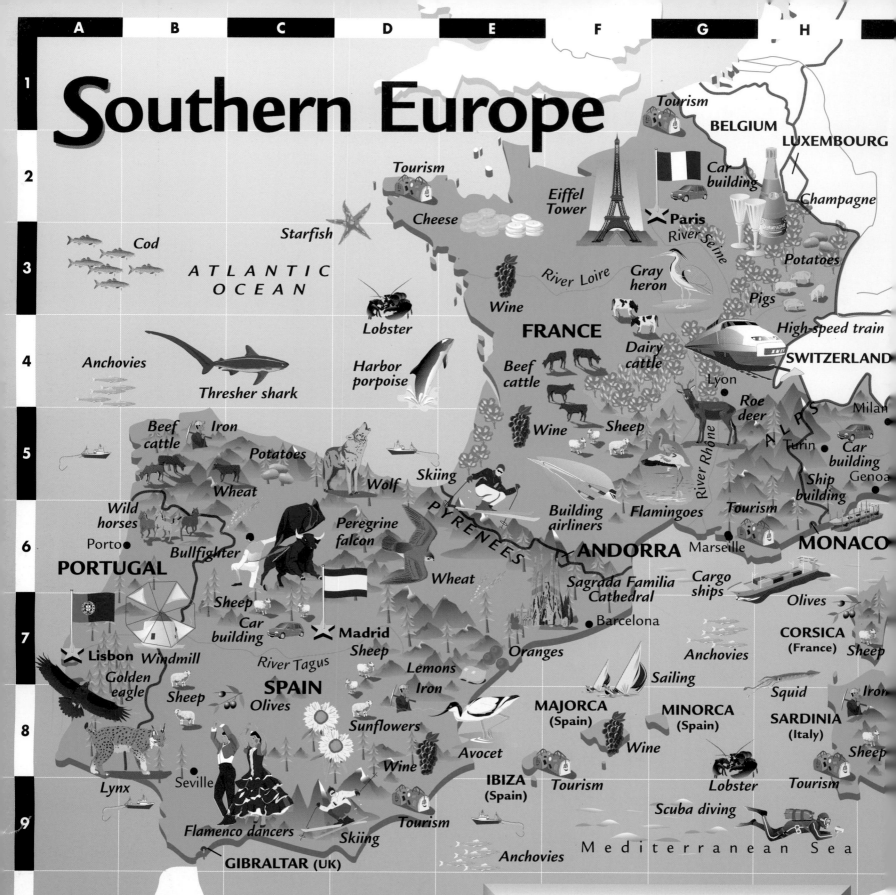

Southern Europe

1

2

3

BELGIUM

LUXEMBOURG

Tourism

Eiffel Tower

Car building

Champagne

Paris

River Seine

Potatoes

ATLANTIC OCEAN

Cod

Starfish

Cheese

River Loire

Gray heron

Pigs

High-speed train

SWITZERLAND

4

Anchovies

Thresher shark

Lobster

Harbor porpoise

FRANCE

Beef cattle

Dairy cattle

Wine

Lyon

Roe deer

Milan

5

Beef cattle

Iron

Potatoes

Wheat

Wild horses

Porto

Bullfighter

Wolf

Skiing

Wine

Sheep

River Rhône

Turin

Car building

Genoa

Ship building

6

Peregrine falcon

Building airliners

Flamingoes

Tourism

ANDORRA

Marseille

MONACO

PORTUGAL

Sheep

Car building

Madrid

Wheat

Sagrada Familia Cathedral

Cargo ships

Olives

7

Lisbon

Windmill

Golden eagle

Sheep

Olives

SPAIN

River Tagus

Sheep

Lemons

Iron

Oranges

Barcelona

Anchovies

Sailing

Squid

CORSICA (France)

Sheep

Iron

8

Lynx

Seville

Sunflowers

Wine

Avocet

MAJORCA (Spain)

Wine

MINORCA (Spain)

SARDINIA (Italy)

Sheep

9

Flamenco dancers

Skiing

Tourism

IBIZA (Spain)

Tourism

Lobster

Tourism

Scuba diving

GIBRALTAR (UK)

Anchovies

M e d i t e r r a n e a n   S e a

10

11

12

13

Southern Europe is warm, sunny and mainly dry. Large parts of it are covered with mountains and hills, but there is still plenty of good farmland. Many people in southern Europe are farmers. They grow cereals and all kinds of fruit and vegetables. Southern Europe also has many famous ancient buildings and works of art. Each year millions of tourists visit its museums and art galleries.

👉 FACT FINDER

▶ Which Italian bell tower, built over 300 years ago, began to lean before it was even finished? (See square I 6.)

▶ What is the name of the ancient Roman stadium where gladiators once fought with swords and nets? (See J 7.)

▶ Which ancient Greek temple was built to worship the goddess Athene, protector of Athens? (See square N 8.)

Factfile

Mount Etna in Sicily is the largest volcano in Europe. It last erupted in 1995.

Spain produces more olive oil than any other country. Each year it produces enough olive oil to fill 160 Olympic-sized swimming pools.

Russia and its neighbors

Grid columns: A B C D E F G H

Grid rows: 1 2 3 4 5 6 7 8 9 10 11 12 13

EUROPE

ARCTIC OCEAN

SWEDEN

FINLAND

Arctic Circle

Ice breakers

Murmansk

Reindeer

Ice breakers

Kaliningrad (Russia)

St Petersburg

Russian dolls

Archangel

Forestry

Snowy owl

Winter camp of Nentsy people

Badger

Forestry

Potatoes

Coal

Gas

Gas

Minsk

BELARUS

Moscow

Bolshoi Ballet

URAL MOUNTAINS

Wolf

Gas

Kishinev

Sugar beet

Kiev

St Basil's Cathedral

Nizhniy Novgorod

Car building

Oil

River Ob

Oil

MOLDOVA

UKRAINE

Potatoes

River Don

Sugar beet

Tractor building

Barley

Gold

R U S

Tourism

Black Sea

Corn

Coal

River Volga

Oil

Iron

Wheat

Hamster

Wine

Volgograd

Pigs

S t e p p e

TURKEY

GEORGIA

Mt Elbrus

Wheat

Pelican

Crane

Baykonur Cosmodrome

Beef cattle

Coal

Tbilisi

Sturgeon

KAZAKHSTAN

ARMENIA

Yerevan

Oil

Iron

Copper

River Irtysh

AZERBAIJAN

Caspian Sea

Aral Sea

Gymnastics

Sunflowers

Cotton

Baku

Cotton

UZBEKISTAN

Tobacco

Kara Kum Desert

Gas

Gas

Cotton

Bishkek

Alma-Ata

Gas

Carpet weaving

Tashkent

KYRGYZSTA

Ashgabat

River Amu Darya

Dushanbe

Wild horses

Cotton

TURKMENISTAN

Oil

TAJIKISTAN

A S I A

FACT FINDER

▶ Which space center launched the world's first astronaut, Yuri Gagarin, into space in 1961? (See square G 8.)

▶ Which Russian railway line is the longest railway line in the world? It takes seven days to travel along it from one end to the other. (See square J 8.)

This distance is the same as 700 miles (1,100km) on the ground.

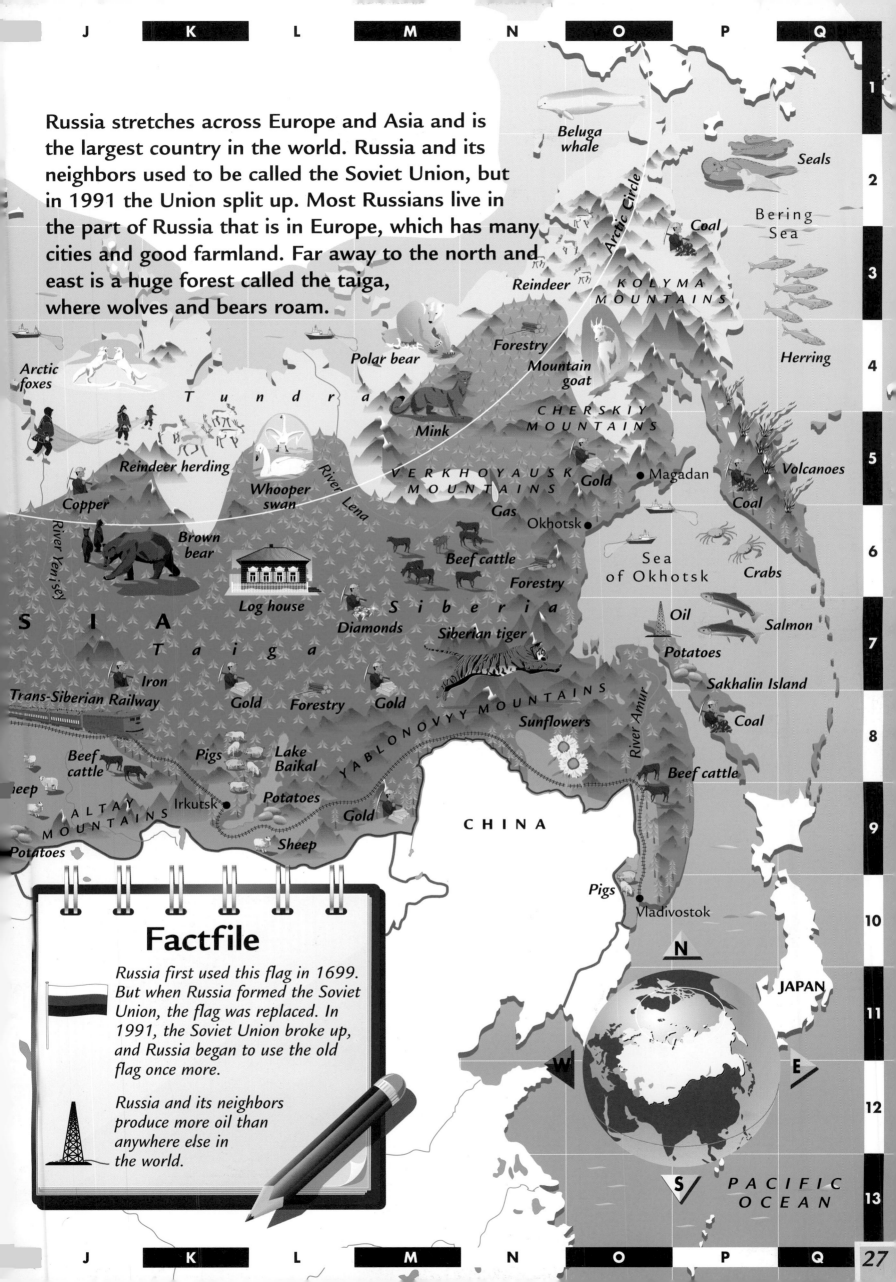

Russia stretches across Europe and Asia and is the largest country in the world. Russia and its neighbors used to be called the Soviet Union, but in 1991 the Union split up. Most Russians live in the part of Russia that is in Europe, which has many cities and good farmland. Far away to the north and east is a huge forest called the taiga, where wolves and bears roam.

Beluga whale

Seals

Bering Sea

Coal

Arctic Circle

Reindeer

K O L Y M A
M O U N T A I N S

Herring

Forestry

Mountain goat

Polar bear

Arctic foxes

T u n d r a

C H E R S K I Y
M O U N T A I N S

Mink

Reindeer herding

Whooper swan

River Lena

V E R K H O Y A U S K
M O U N T A I N S

Gold

Magadan

Volcanoes

Copper

Gas

Okhotsk

Coal

River Yenisey

Brown bear

Log house

Beef cattle

Sea of Okhotsk

Crabs

S I A

Forestry

Diamonds

S i b e r i a

Siberian tiger

Oil

Salmon

Potatoes

T a i g a

Iron

Gold

Forestry

Gold

Y A B L O N O V Y Y   M O U N T A I N S

Sunflowers

River Amur

Sakhalin Island

Coal

Trans-Siberian Railway

Beef cattle

Pigs

Lake Baikal

Potatoes

Sheep

Gold

C H I N A

Beef cattle

Irkutsk

A L T A Y
M O U N T A I N S

Sheep

Pigs

Vladivostok

Potatoes

N

Factfile

Russia first used this flag in 1699. But when Russia formed the Soviet Union, the flag was replaced. In 1991, the Soviet Union broke up, and Russia began to use the old flag once more.

Russia and its neighbors produce more oil than anywhere else in the world.

W

E

JAPAN

S

P A C I F I C
O C E A N

Southwest Asia

The southwest corner of Asia is also called the Middle East. Here, thousands of years ago, people first became farmers, then settled close together in towns. Much of the land in southwest Asia is hot, dry desert, which can be hard to farm. Fifty years ago, people found oil under the desert. They used the money they made from the oil to build huge watering systems, so they could grow crops more easily in the poor soil. They also built large cities.

Factfile

Over 5,000 years ago, the first cities in the world grew up in southwest Asia, along the Tigris and Euphrates Rivers.

Three of the world's major religions began in southwest Asia. They are Islam, Judaism and Christianity.

Southwest Asia makes some of the world's most expensive hand-made carpets. Carpet-makers weave and knot wool to make different patterns which can tell you the area the carpet comes from.

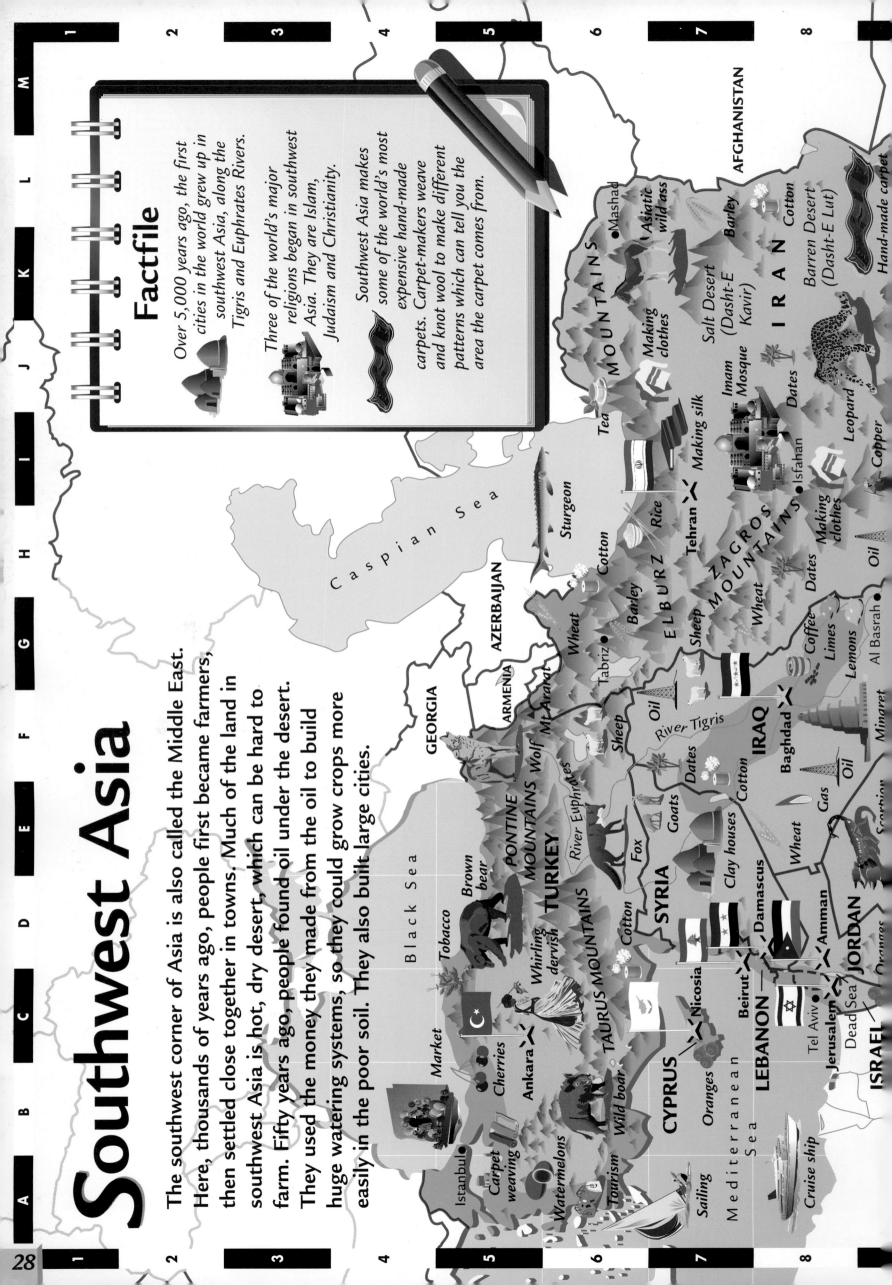

Caspian Sea

Black Sea

Mediterranean Sea

GEORGIA

ARMENIA

AZERBAIJAN

TURKEY
Ankara•

Istanbul•

PONTINE MOUNTAINS

TAURUS MOUNTAINS

Mt Ararat

River Euphrates

CYPRUS
Nicosia•

LEBANON
Beirut•

SYRIA
Damascus•

ISRAEL
Tel Aviv•
Jerusalem•
Dead Sea

JORDAN
Amman•

IRAQ
Baghdad•
River Tigris
Al Basrah•

IRAN
Tehran•
Tabriz•
Isfahan•
Mashad•

ELBURZ MOUNTAINS

ZAGROS MOUNTAINS

Salt Desert (Dasht-E Kavir)

Barren Desert (Dasht-E Lut)

AFGHANISTAN

Imam Mosque

Labels on the map:
- Carpet weaving
- Sailing
- Oranges
- Watermelons
- Tourism
- Wild boar
- Cherries
- Market
- Tobacco
- Brown bear
- Whirling dervish
- Cotton
- Wolf
- Fox
- Goats
- Dates
- Clay houses
- Wheat
- Gas
- Oil
- Cotton
- Minaret
- Scorpion
- Oranges
- Sheep
- Wheat
- Barley
- Cotton
- Oil
- Sturgeon
- Rice
- Tea
- Making clothes
- Making silk
- Asiatic wild ass
- Barley
- Dates
- Wheat
- Making clothes
- Dates
- Leopard
- Copper
- Oil
- Cotton
- Hand-made carpet
- Coffee
- Limes
- Lemons
- Cruise ship

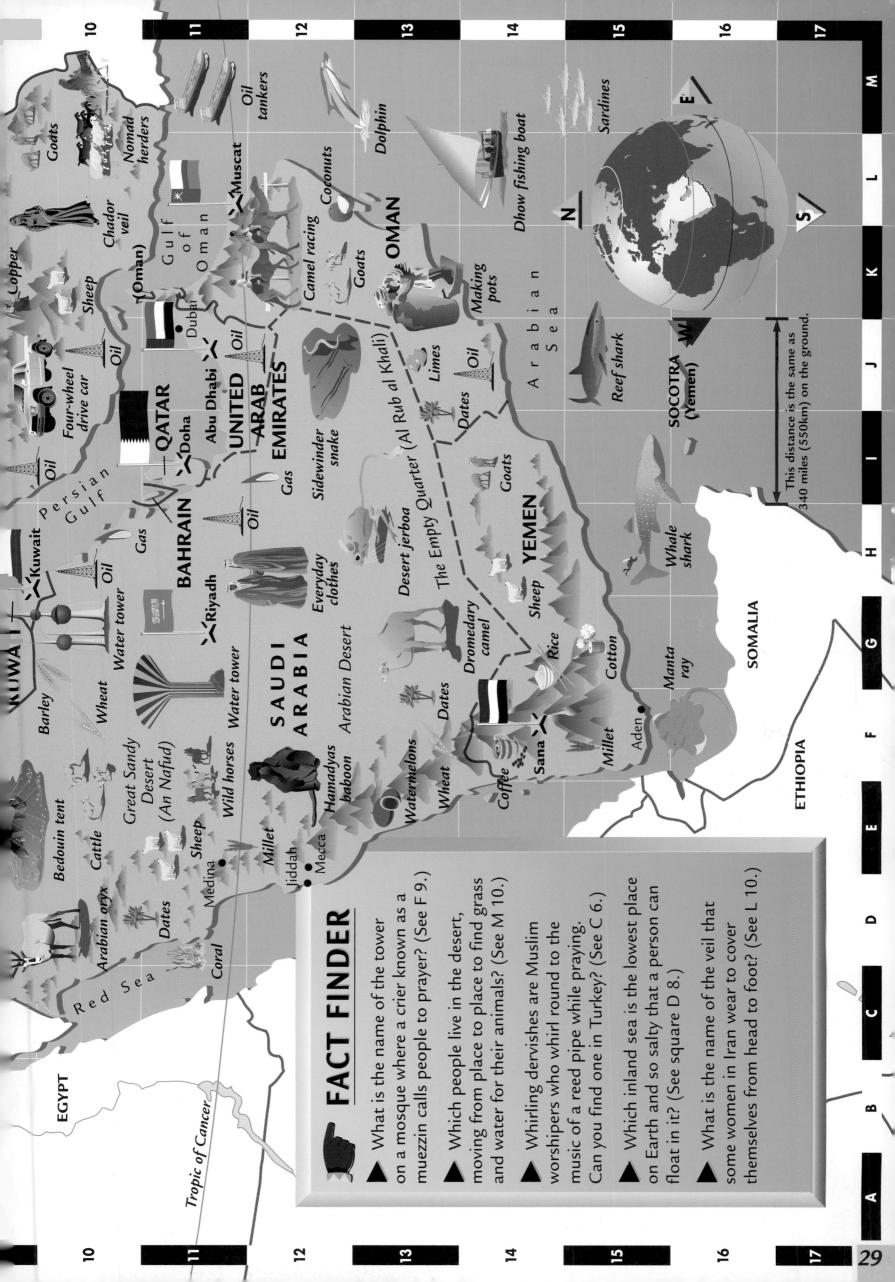

FACT FINDER

▲ What is the name of the tower on a mosque where a crier known as a muezzin calls people to prayer? (See F 9.)

▲ Which people live in the desert, moving from place to place to find grass and water for their animals? (See M 10.)

▲ Whirling dervishes are Muslim worshipers who whirl round to the music of a reed pipe while praying. Can you find one in Turkey? (See C 6.)

▲ Which inland sea is the lowest place on Earth and so salty that a person can float in it? (See square D 8.)

▲ What is the name of the veil that some women in Iran wear to cover themselves from head to foot? (See L 10.)

This distance is the same as 340 miles (550km) on the ground.

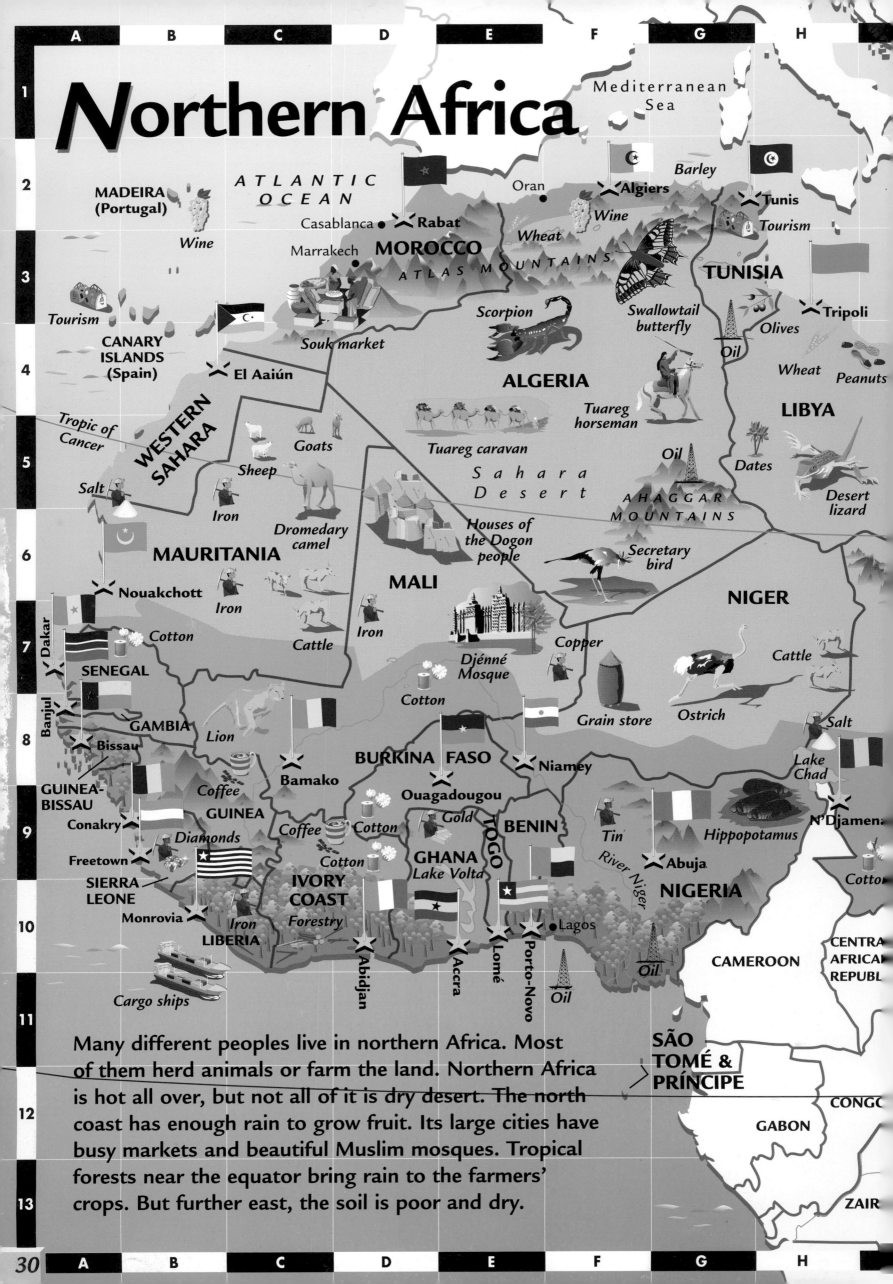

Northern Africa

Mediterranean Sea

ATLANTIC OCEAN

MADEIRA (Portugal)

Wine

Tourism

CANARY ISLANDS (Spain)

Tropic of Cancer

Oran

Barley

Algiers

Wine

Wine

Wheat

Casablanca

Rabat

Marrakech

MOROCCO

ATLAS MOUNTAINS

Souk market

Tunis

Tourism

TUNISIA

Tripoli

Olives

Oil

Wheat

Peanuts

LIBYA

Scorpion

ALGERIA

Swallowtail butterfly

Tuareg horseman

Dates

Oil

El Aaiún

WESTERN SAHARA

Salt

Sheep

Goats

Iron

Dromedary camel

Tuareg caravan

Sahara Desert

AHAGGAR MOUNTAINS

Desert lizard

MAURITANIA

Iron

Nouakchott

Iron

Cattle

Iron

MALI

Houses of the Dogon people

Secretary bird

NIGER

Dakar

Cotton

SENEGAL

Banjul

GAMBIA

Lion

Bissau

GUINEA-BISSAU

Conakry

Diamonds

Coffee

GUINEA

Coffee

Bamako

Cotton

Djénné Mosque

Cotton

Copper

Grain store

Ostrich

Cattle

Salt

Lake Chad

N'Djamena

Freetown

SIERRA LEONE

Monrovia

Iron

LIBERIA

Forestry

Cotton

IVORY COAST

Cotton

BURKINA FASO

Ouagadougou

Gold

GHANA

Lake Volta

TOGO

BENIN

Tin

River Niger

Niamey

Hippopotamus

Abuja

NIGERIA

Cotton

Cargo ships

Abidjan

Accra

Lomé

Porto-Novo

Lagos

Oil

Oil

CAMEROON

CENTRAL AFRICAN REPUBLIC

SÃO TOMÉ & PRÍNCIPE

GABON

CONGO

ZAIR

Many different peoples live in northern Africa. Most of them herd animals or farm the land. Northern Africa is hot all over, but not all of it is dry desert. The north coast has enough rain to grow fruit. Its large cities have busy markets and beautiful Muslim mosques. Tropical forests near the equator bring rain to the farmers' crops. But further east, the soil is poor and dry.

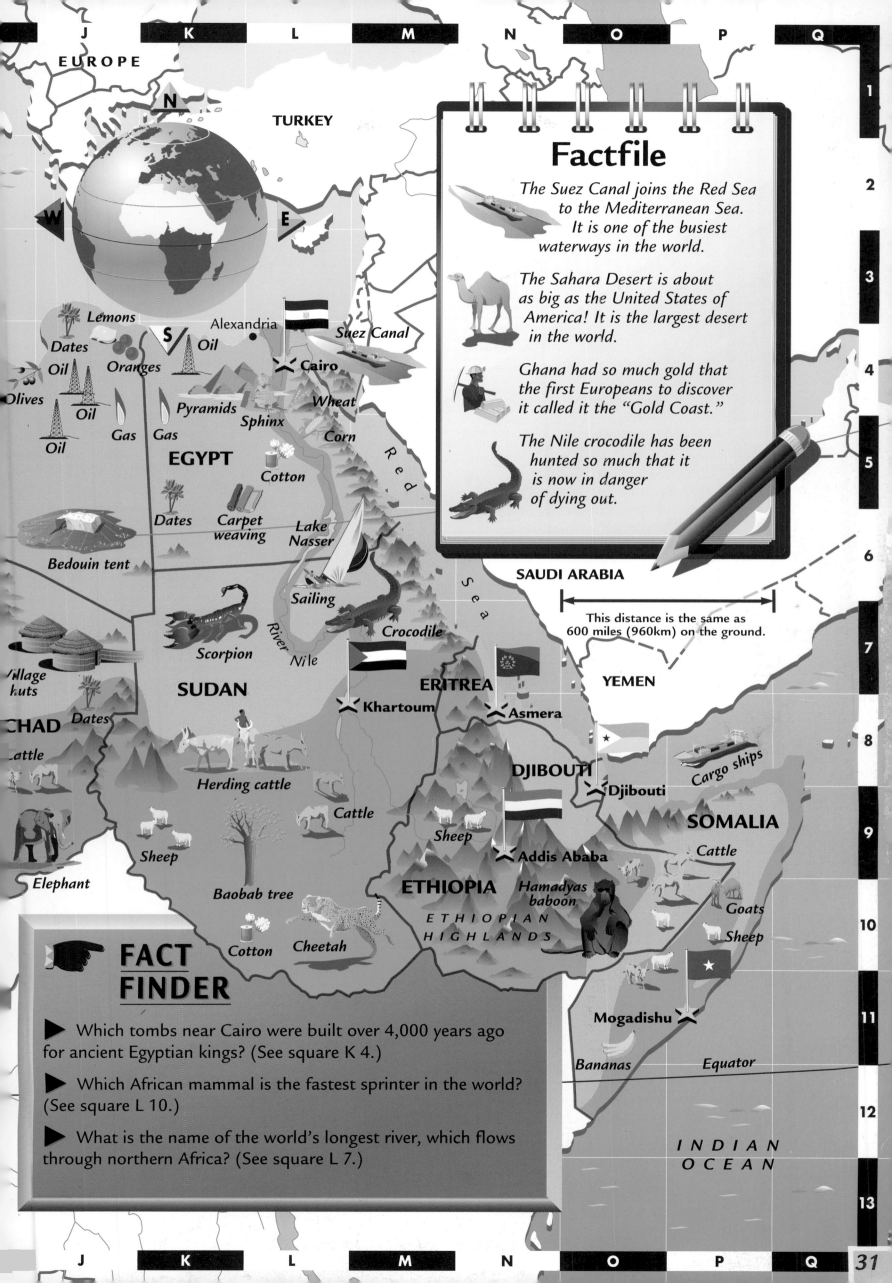

EUROPE

J K L M N O P Q

TURKEY

Factfile

The Suez Canal joins the Red Sea to the Mediterranean Sea. It is one of the busiest waterways in the world.

The Sahara Desert is about as big as the United States of America! It is the largest desert in the world.

Ghana had so much gold that the first Europeans to discover it called it the "Gold Coast."

The Nile crocodile has been hunted so much that it is now in danger of dying out.

Lemons

Alexandria

Dates
Oil   Oil

Oil   Oranges

Olives

Oil   Suez Canal

Cairo

Oil
Gas   Gas

Pyramids

Sphinx

Wheat

EGYPT

Corn

Cotton

Red

SAUDI ARABIA

Dates   Carpet weaving

Lake Nasser

Bedouin tent

Sailing

This distance is the same as 600 miles (960km) on the ground.

Scorpion

Crocodile

YEMEN

River Nile

SUDAN

ERITREA

Khartoum

Asmera

Village huts

CHAD   Dates

Cattle

Herding cattle

DJIBOUTI

Djibouti

Cargo ships

Cattle

SOMALIA

Cattle

Sheep

Addis Ababa

Elephant

Sheep

Baobab tree

ETHIOPIA

Hamadyas baboon

Goats

E T H I O P I A N
H I G H L A N D S

Sheep

Cotton   Cheetah

Mogadishu

Bananas   Equator

FACT FINDER

▶ Which tombs near Cairo were built over 4,000 years ago for ancient Egyptian kings? (See square K 4.)

▶ Which African mammal is the fastest sprinter in the world? (See square L 10.)

▶ What is the name of the world's longest river, which flows through northern Africa? (See square L 7.)

I N D I A N
O C E A N

J K L M N O P Q

Southern Africa

Southern Africa is a vast land of grasslands, rainforests, mountains and deserts. The plains of Kenya and Tanzania are famous for their huge herds of animals. Further west, in the rainforests, there are gorillas, monkeys and tropical birds. Many different peoples live in Africa. Most of them farm in small villages, but the cities are growing. Many countries mine copper and gold. Some mine diamonds too.

Factfile

Southern Africa is home to the black rhino and the mountain gorilla, two of the world's most endangered animals.

Southern Africa has large areas of rainforest. Altogether, about one quarter of the world's forests grow in southern Africa.

South Africa is the world's largest producer of gold.

This distance is the same as 450 miles (725km) on the ground.

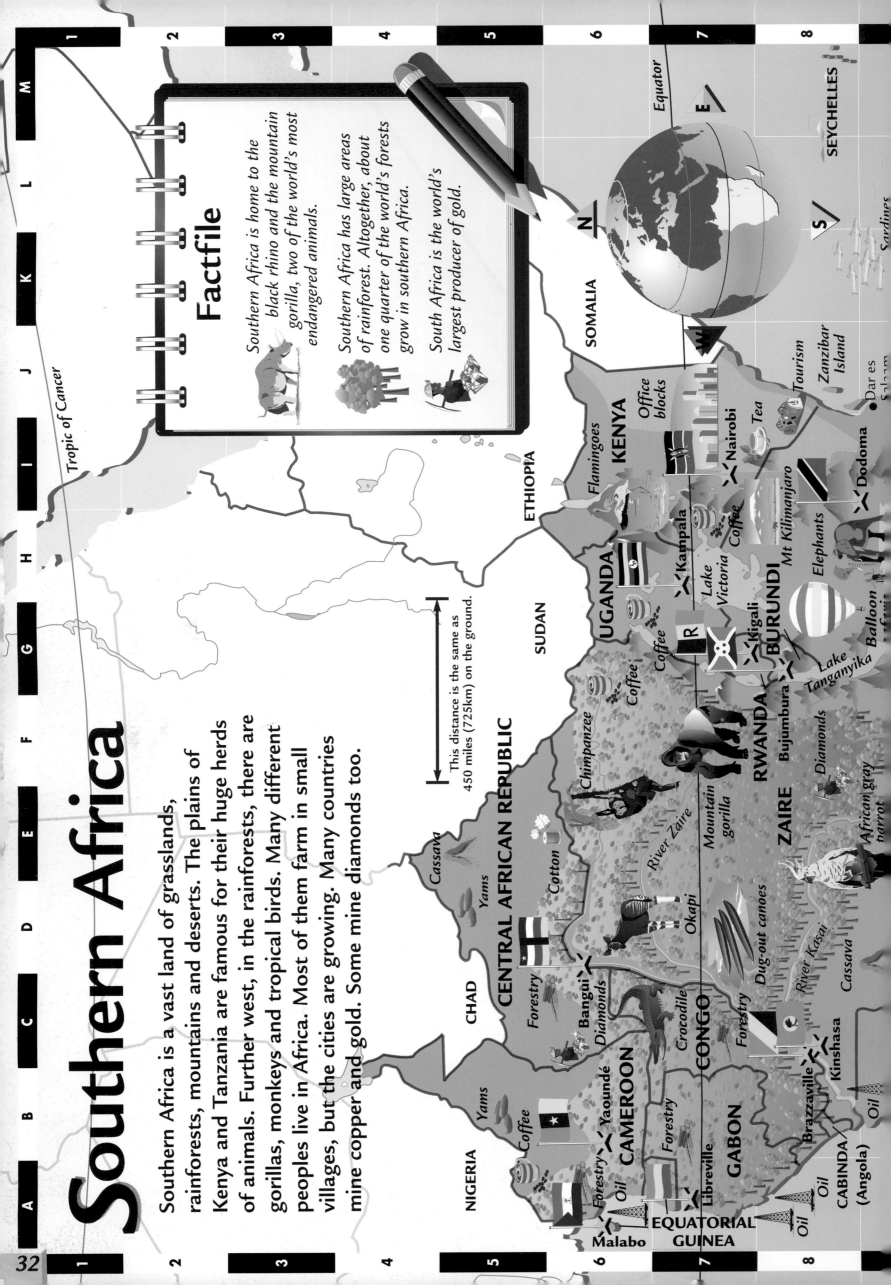

Tropic of Cancer

Equator

N
W
S

NIGERIA
Yams
Coffee
Oil

CAMEROON
Yaoundé
Forestry

EQUATORIAL GUINEA
Malabo
Oil

GABON
Libreville
Forestry
Brazzaville
Oil

CABINDA (Angola)
Oil

CONGO
Forestry
Kinshasa

CHAD

CENTRAL AFRICAN REPUBLIC
Bangui
Diamonds
Forestry
Cassava
Yams
Cotton
Crocodile
Okapi

SUDAN

ETHIOPIA

SOMALIA

UGANDA
Kampala
Coffee

KENYA
Nairobi
Office blocks
Tea
Coffee
Flamingoes
Mt Kilimanjaro
Elephants

Lake Victoria

RWANDA
Kigali

BURUNDI
Bujumbura

ZAIRE
Chimpanzee
River Zaïre
Mountain gorilla
Dug-out canoes
River Kasai
Cassava
Diamonds
African gray parrot

Lake Tanganyika
Balloon

Dodoma

Tourism
Zanzibar Island
Dar es Salaam

SEYCHELLES

Sardines

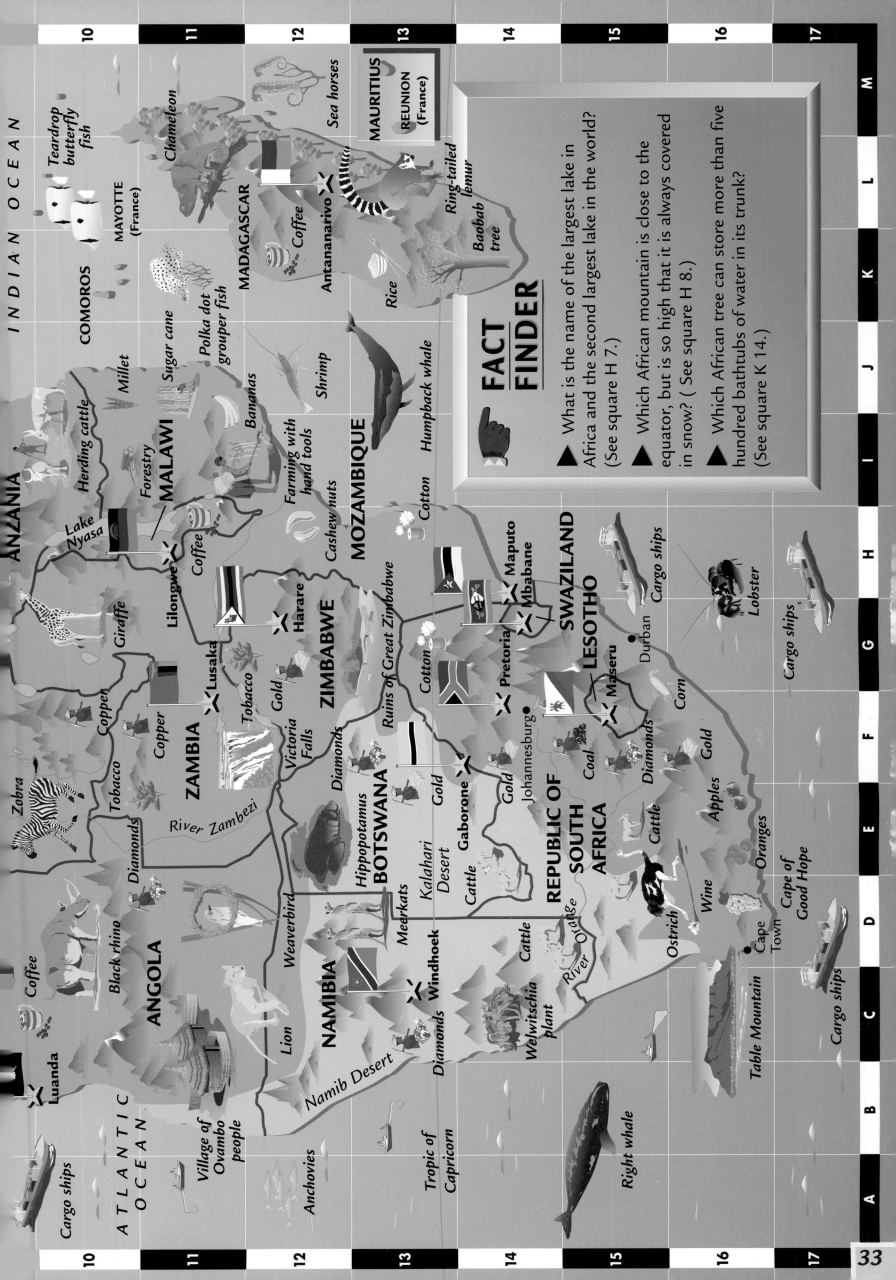

INDIAN OCEAN

ATLANTIC OCEAN

COMOROS

MAYOTTE (France)

Teardrop butterfly fish

Chameleon

Sea horses

MAURITIUS

REUNION (France)

MADAGASCAR

Coffee

Ring-tailed lemur

Baobab tree

Antananarivo

Rice

Polka dot grouper fish

Sugar cane

Millet

Shrimp

Bananas

Herding cattle

Forestry

MALAWI

Lake Nyasa

Lilongwe

Coffee

Cashew nuts

Farming with hand tools

MOZAMBIQUE

Humpback whale

Cotton

TANZANIA

Giraffe

Copper

Zebra

Black rhino

Coffee

Luanda

Cargo ships

ANGOLA

Village of Ovambo people

Lion

Copper

Tobacco

Diamonds

Tobacco

Gold

Harare

ZIMBABWE

Victoria Falls

ZAMBIA

Lusaka

River Zambezi

Ruins of Great Zimbabwe

Diamonds

Hippopotamus

BOTSWANA

Gold

Gaborone

Cattle

Kalahari Desert

Cotton

Cotton

SWAZILAND

Maputo
Mbabane

Pretoria

LESOTHO

Maseru

Durban

Cargo ships

Lobster

Cargo ships

Johannesburg

REPUBLIC OF SOUTH AFRICA

Coal

Corn

Diamonds

Gold

Cattle

Apples

Gold

Wine

Oranges

Ostrich

Cape Town

Cape of Good Hope

Table Mountain

Cargo ships

Right whale

Tropic of Capricorn

Anchovies

Namib Desert

NAMIBIA

Windhoek

Diamonds

Welwitschia plant

River Orange

Cattle

Cattle

Weaverbird

Meerkats

Diamonds

FACT FINDER

▲ What is the name of the largest lake in Africa and the second largest lake in the world? (See square H 7.)

▲ Which African mountain is close to the equator, but is so high that it is always covered in snow? (See square H 8.)

▲ Which African tree can store more than five hundred bathtubs of water in its trunk? (See square K 14.)

Southern Asia

Southern Asia stretches from the Himalayan Mountains in the north of India to the island of Sri Lanka in the south. The weather is mostly hot and dry, although for several months there are heavy rains. More than a billion people live in southern Asia. Most people live in villages and farm the land, but many are beginning to move to the cities. The cities are a mixture of old and new, with modern buildings next to ancient temples and palaces. The busy streets are packed with cars, trucks and buses, but also with ox-carts and elephants.

☞ FACT FINDER

▲ Which white marble temple, decorated with precious stones, was built in the 17th century by an Indian emperor as a burial place for his wife? (See square G 8.)

▲ In India, which animal is used to help people with heavy work such as moving timber? (See square F 11.)

▲ What are Pakistan, Afghanistan and India all famous for weaving? (See squares C 6, C 9 and F 7.)

▲ In India, which three-wheeled vehicle that looks a little like a bicycle is often used to carry people from one place to another? (See square I 10.)

TURKMENISTAN

UZBEKISTAN

TAJIKISTAN

AFGHANISTAN

Bactrian camel

Milking goats

River Helmand

Cotton

Wheat

Blue Mosque

Cattle

Kabul

Carpet weaving

Rubies

Peaches

Goats

Cotton

Quetta

PAKISTAN

Wheat

Goats

River Indus

Shah Faisal Mosque

Islamabad

Sugar cane

Lahore

Wheat

Cobra

Cattle

Thar

KARAKORAM RANGE

Snow leopard

Carpet weaving

Wheat

Making

Delhi

Taj Mahal

HIMALAYAN MOUNTAINS

Goats

Mountain peaks

Mt Everest

Yak

CHINA

NEPAL

Kathmandu

Sugar cane

Rice

Tea

BHUTAN

Thimpu

River Brahmaputra

Tea

Oil

Buddhist monk

Indian rhino

MYANMAR

BANGLADESH
Dhaka
Chittagong
Calcutta
Making silk
Car building
Crocodile
Iron

River Ganges

INDIA

Forestry
Peacock
VINHDAYA RANGE
River Narmada
Oil
Making clothes
Film making
Bombay
Steam train

Wheat
Ahmadabad
Sheep
Dromedary camels
Peanuts
Cotton
Carpet weaving
Oil
Karachi
Film making

Millet
Tropic of Cancer
Herring

Dhow fishing boat

This distance is the same as 360 miles (575km) on the ground.

Blue whale

Coal
Bicycle rickshaw
Rice
Rice
Black bear
Nagpur
Working elephant
River Godavari
Cotton
Hyderabad
Coal
Black panther
Iron
Gold
Bangalore
Cochin
Cattle
Ship building
Shrimp
Tiger
Car building
Madras
Rice
Coconuts
Colombo
Tea
Pearls

Water buffalo

Classical Indian dancing

Millet
Tourism
Goods truck

Vishakhapatnam
Rice

Reef shark
Lobster

ANDAMAN ISLANDS (India)

Dolphins

Polka dot grouper fish

Humpback whale

INDIAN OCEAN

Coral
NICOBAR ISLANDS (India)

N
W
E
S

SRI LANKA

Sardines

Scuba diving
Coral
Clown fish

MALDIVE ISLANDS

Outrigger fishing boat

Equator

Factfile

More films are made in southern Asia than anywhere else in the world. India makes over 700 films a year.

The mountains of southern Asia are home to the snow leopard, one of the world's most endangered animals.

Southern Asia is the world's largest producer of tea.

Eastern Asia

Eastern Asia is made up of China, Mongolia, Japan, North and South Korea, Taiwan and Hong Kong. It is a vast land with mountains and deserts in the north and west. Most people live further east, where there is more rain and good farmland. China is a huge country. Many people are farmers and live in the countryside. In Japan, most people live in cities. They work in factories and offices.

RUSSIA

This distance is the same as 280 miles (450km) on the ground.

Goats

Red deer

Ulan Bator

ALTAI MOUNTAINS

TIEN SHAN MOUNTAINS

Wolf

Yurt

Coal

M O N G

Oil

Copper

Cotton

Goats

Gob

Rice

Iron

Wheat

Sheep

Bactrian camel

Wild horses

Cotton

Sand grouse

Oil

Sheep

Wild horses

Cotton

Takla Makan Desert

Cotton

Great Wall of China

PAKISTAN

Gas

Vulture

Oil

K2 (Mt Godwin Austen)

Tai Chi exercises

Calligraphy

Wild boar

Salt mining

T I B E T

Snow leopard

INDIA

Yak

Cattle

Goats

Sheep

C H I N A

HIMALAYAN MOUNTAINS

Buddhist monk

Pigs

Chengdu

Mountain peaks

Potala Palace

▲ Mt Everest

Great Buddha

BHUTAN

INDIA

N

MYANMAR

Stone forest

W

E

Tobacco

LAOS

S

Tea

THAILAND

FACT FINDER

► Which ancient exercises do many Chinese people perform every morning to keep themselves healthy? (See E 7.)

► Which wall is about 4,000 miles (6,400km) long and was built over 500 years ago to protect China from northern invaders? (See square H 6.)

► What is the name of the tent traveling herders in Mongolia live in to protect themselves from the heat and cold of the plains? (See square G 3.)

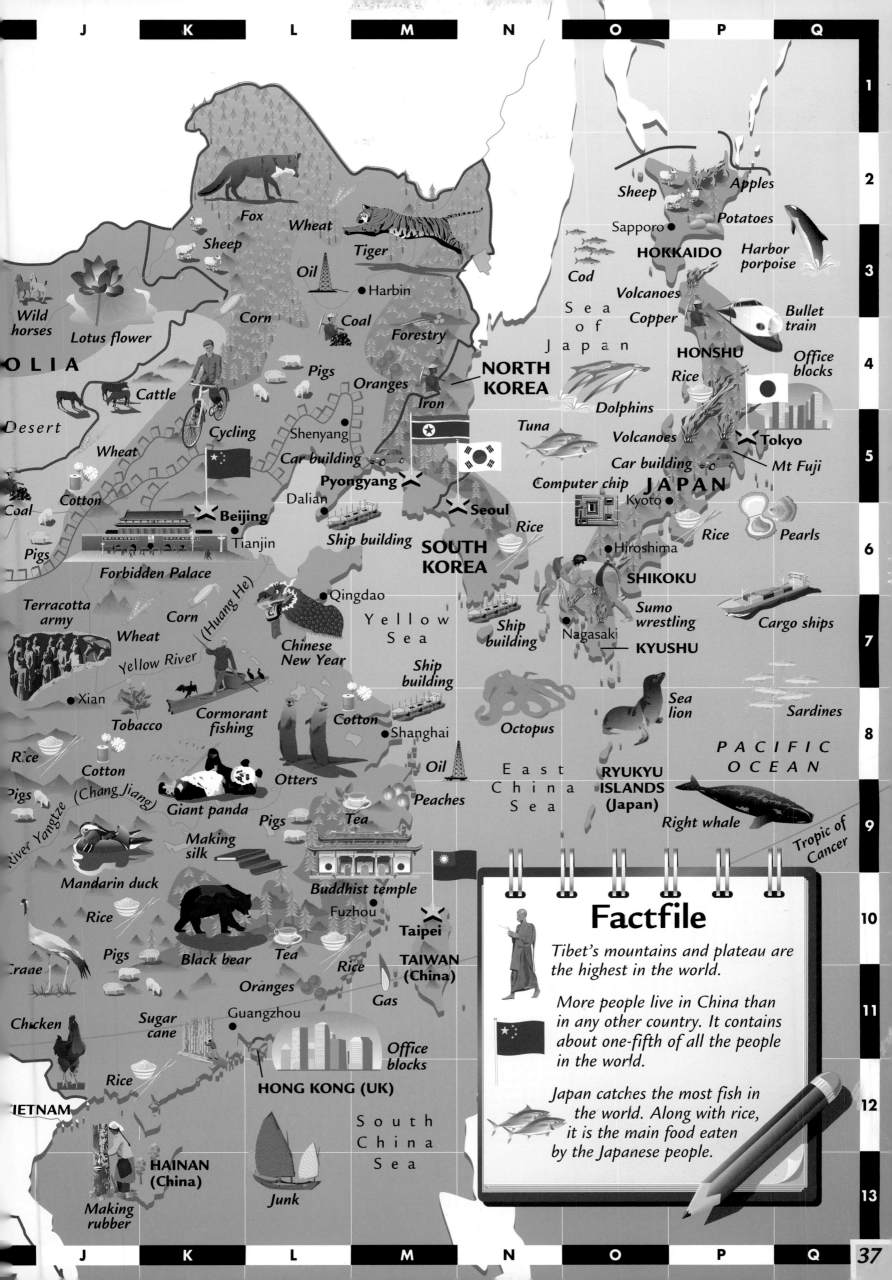

1
2
3
4
5
6
7
8
9
10
11
12
13

Fox
Wheat
Sheep
Tiger
Oil
• Harbin
Corn
Coal
Forestry
Wild horses
Lotus flower
OLIA
Desert
Cattle
Cycling
Wheat
Shenyang •
Pigs
Oranges
Iron
Car building
Cotton
Dalian •
Coal
Pyongyang
Beijing
Pigs
• Tianjin
Forbidden Palace
Terracotta army
Corn
Qingdao •
Wheat
(Huang He)
Yellow River
Chinese New Year
Xian •
Tobacco
Cormorant fishing
Cotton
Rice
Shanghai •
Cotton
(Chang Jiang)
Oil
Giant panda
Otters
Peaches
Pigs
River Yangtze
Mandarin duck
Making silk
Tea
Rice
Buddhist temple
Crane
Pigs
Black bear
Tea
Fuzhou •
Rice
Taipei
Oranges
Gas
TAIWAN (China)
Chicken
Sugar cane
Guangzhou •
Rice
Office blocks
VIETNAM
HONG KONG (UK)
HAINAN (China)
South China Sea
Junk
Making rubber

Sheep
Apples
Sapporo •
Potatoes
HOKKAIDO
Harbor porpoise
Cod
Volcanoes
Sea of Japan
Copper
Bullet train
NORTH KOREA
HONSHU
Rice
Office blocks
Dolphins
Tuna
Volcanoes
Tokyo
Car building
Mt Fuji
Computer chip
JAPAN
SOUTH KOREA
Kyoto •
Seoul
Ship building
Rice
• Hiroshima
Rice
Pearls
SHIKOKU
Sumo wrestling
Ship building
Nagasaki •
KYUSHU
Cargo ships
Yellow Sea
Ship building
Sea lion
Octopus
Sardines
PACIFIC OCEAN
East China Sea
RYUKYU ISLANDS (Japan)
Right whale
Tropic of Cancer

Factfile

Tibet's mountains and plateau are the highest in the world.

More people live in China than in any other country. It contains about one-fifth of all the people in the world.

Japan catches the most fish in the world. Along with rice, it is the main food eaten by the Japanese people.

Southeast Asia

TAIWAN

Scuba diving

CHINA

Tropic of Cancer

Coal

Clown fish

Coral

Stilt house

Wild boar
MYANMAR

Water buffalo

Hanoi

LUZON

Working elephant

LAOS

Tiger

S o u t h
C h i n a
S e a

Coral

Copper

Manila

Rice

Vientiane

River Mekong

VIETNAM

Coral

PHILIP

River Irrawaddy

THAILAND

Making silk

Cassava

Herring

Coral

Silver

Rice

Floating market

Rice

Anchovies

Sardines

Gold

Yangon

Bangkok

Corn

Pearls

Oil

Reef sharks

I N D I A N
O C E A N

Angkor Wat

Phnom Penh

• **Ho Chi Minh City**

CAMBODIA

Rice

Tuna

Leatherback turtle

BRUNEI

Bandar Seri Begawan

Lobster

Gas

Oil

Making rubber

Rice

Polka dot grouper fish

Malayan tapir

Tourism

Iron

M A L A Y S I A

Forestry

Orang-utan

Gas

Coral

Tourism
Kuala Lumpur

Office blocks

SINGAPORE

BORNEO

Oil

Forestry

I N D O

Volcanoes

SUMATRA

Oil

Cargo ships

Orchid

FACT FINDER

▶ What is the name of the world's largest lizard? It can grow more than 10 feet (3m) long and lives only in Indonesia. (See square J 11.)

▶ Which temple in Cambodia is one of the architectural wonders of the world? It was built over 800 years ago to honor the Hindu god, Vishnu. (See square D 7.)

Gas

Volcanoes

Rafflesia flower

Jakarta **JAVA**

Volcanoes

Tea

Sea horses

Teardrop butterfly fish

Coral

Southeast Asia is made up of a narrow strip of land and thousands of small islands. The area has high mountains, tropical forests and river valleys. The weather is hot and wet all year round. Many of the people are farmers, who grow rice and corn for food, and rubber and coffee to sell. But the cities are growing, and more people are finding work in factories and offices.

This distance is the same as 500 miles (800km) on the ground.

Factfile

Rubber is made from the sap of the rubber tree. Southeast Asia produces over three-quarters of the world's rubber.

There are more active volcanoes in southeast Asia than in any other area of the world. The ash left behind from volcanic eruptions helps to make the soil good for farming.

The country of Indonesia is made up of over 13,600 islands. It is the biggest chain of islands in the world and has the world's fourth largest population.

Bicycle rickshaw

PINES

Coconuts

MINDANAO

Outrigger fishing boat

NORTH PACIFIC OCEAN

Equator

Tuna

Bird of paradise

Coconuts

Sponge

Gas Oil

IRIAN JAYA (Indonesia)

PAPUA NEW GUINEA

Coconuts

MALUKU

Shrimp

Bananas

Cloves

Tree kangaroo

Echidna

Port Moresby

SULAWESI

Flying lizard

Crab

Humpback whale

Coffee

NESIA

Manta ray

Komodo dragon

FLORES

TIMOR

N E

BALI

SUMBA

Shrimp

Tourism

AUSTRALIA

Dolphins

Tropic of Capricorn

1
2
3
4
5
6
7
8
9
10
11
12
13

Australia, New Zealand
and the Pacific Islands

The Pacific Ocean is dotted with thousands of islands. Many people live in villages and grow crops or hunt for fish. Australia is an island too, but it is so big that it is a continent. Most Australians live in cities or farm land near the coast. A lot of Australia is hot and dry, but it has mountains and rainforests too. It also has animals and plants that are not found anywhere else.

Shrimp

Darwin

Crocodile

Manta ray

Beef cattle

Cattle ranching

Road train

Beef cattle

NORTHERN TERRITORY

Cave paintings

Tanami Desert

Boomerang

Diamonds

A U S T R A L I A

Beef cattle

Baobab tree

● Alice Springs

Uluru (Ayers Rock)

I N D I A N
O C E A N

Iron

Water hole

Tiger snake

Reef sharks

Tropic of Capricorn

Flying Doctor service

ME-LJL

Emu

Sheep

Camels

Dingoes

SOUTH AUSTRALIA

Lake Eyr

Sailing

WESTERN AUSTRALIA

Great Victoria Desert

Opals

Coober Pedy ●

Echidna

Gold

Budgerigar

Wombat

● Perth

Wave Rock

Koala

Orang

Wine

Lobster

Dolphin

Adelaid

FACT FINDER

► Which lake in southern Australia is dry for most of the year and fills with water only after heavy rains? (See square H 8.)

► Which mammal has a furry body and feeds milk to its young, but has a duck's bill and hatches its young from eggs? This mammal is only found in Australia. (See square J 9.)

► Many of Australia's rocks are very old. Can you find one that is shaped like a wave and is over 3,000 million years old? (See square D 9.)

Factfile

The Great Barrier Reef off the east coast of Australia is the biggest coral reef in the world.

Nearly half of the world's 3,000 languages are spoken by people in the Pacific Islands.

Australia is the world's flattest continent.

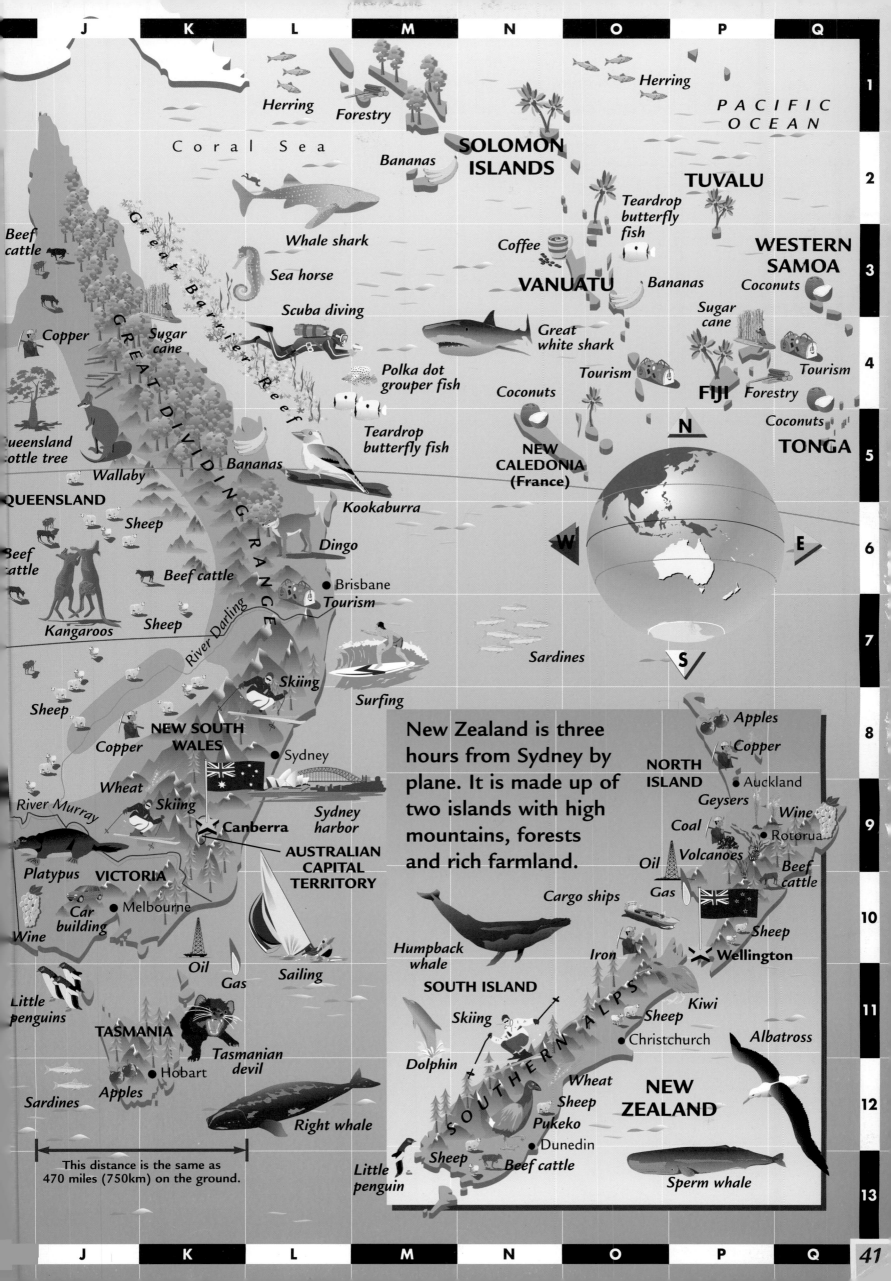

1

Herring

PACIFIC
OCEAN

Herring

Forestry

Coral Sea

2

Bananas

SOLOMON
ISLANDS

TUVALU

Teardrop
butterfly
fish

Beef
cattle

Whale shark

Coffee

WESTERN
SAMOA

3

Sea horse

VANUATU

Bananas

Coconuts

Great
Barrier
Reef

Copper

Sugar
cane

Scuba diving

Sugar
cane

4

GREAT DIVIDING RANGE

Polka dot
grouper fish

Great
white shark

Tourism

Tourism

FIJI

Forestry

Queensland
bottle tree

Coconuts

Coconuts

Teardrop
butterfly fish

N

5

Wallaby

Bananas

NEW
CALEDONIA
(France)

TONGA

QUEENSLAND

Kookaburra

6

Sheep

Beef
cattle

Dingo

W

E

Beef cattle

Brisbane
Tourism

Kangaroos

Sheep

River Darling

S

7

Sheep

Skiing

Surfing

Sardines

8

NEW SOUTH
WALES

Copper

Sydney

New Zealand is three
hours from Sydney by
plane. It is made up of
two islands with high
mountains, forests
and rich farmland.

Apples

Copper

NORTH
ISLAND

Auckland

Wheat

River Murray

Skiing

Sydney
harbor

Geysers

Wine

9

Canberra

Coal

Rotorua

Platypus

VICTORIA

AUSTRALIAN
CAPITAL
TERRITORY

Oil

Volcanoes

Beef
cattle

Car
building

Melbourne

Gas

10

Cargo ships

Wine

Oil

Sheep

Wellington

Gas

Humpback
whale

Iron

Sardines

SOUTH ISLAND

11

Little
penguins

Skiing

Sheep

Kiwi

TASMANIA

Tasmanian
devil

Christchurch

Albatross

Dolphin

Hobart

12

Apples

Wheat

NEW
ZEALAND

Sardines

Right whale

Sheep

This distance is the same as
470 miles (750km) on the ground.

Pukeko

Dunedin

Little
penguin

Sheep

Beef cattle

Sperm whale

13

Fascinating facts

On these pages, you can discover interesting facts about the world. Look up the names of the places in the index and find out where they are on the maps in this atlas.

Where in the world is...

...the hottest place?
Al Aziziyah in Libya. The highest temperature ever recorded was 136°F (58°C).

In Al Aziziyah, you could fry an egg on a sun-baked rock.

...the coldest place?
Vostock in Antarctica. The lowest temperature ever recorded was -129°F. (-89°C). This is over three times as cold as inside a deep freeze.

...the wettest place?
Mawsynram in India, where nearly 40 feet (12m) of rain falls each year. This is enough to cover a three-story building.

...the driest place?
Atacama Desert in Chile, where it has rained only a few times in the last 400 years.

Which country is the...

...biggest country?
Russia, which is 6,592,850 square miles (17,075,400sq km).

...smallest country?
Vatican City, which is 109 acres (44 hectares).

If Russia were the size of a soccer field, the Vatican City would be the size of a small stamp.

...emptiest country?
Mongolia, which has a huge desert and towering mountains. There are only a few towns which are far apart.

...most crowded country?
Monaco, which is a tiny country in Europe. It has an orchestra larger than its army.

Where is the...

...highest mountain in the world?
Mount Everest in the Himalayas, in Nepal. It is about 29,028 ft. (8,848m) high—over nine times as tall as the highest waterfall in the world.

29,028 feet

...highest waterfall in the world?
Angel Falls, in Venezuela. It has a total drop of about 3,212 ft. (979m)—over twice as high as the tallest building in North America.

3,212 feet

...highest building in North America?
Sears Tower, US. It is about 1,454 ft. (443m) tall—nearly four times taller than the tallest geyser in the world.

1,454 feet

...highest geyser in the world?
Steamboat Geyser, US, has reached a height of about 380 ft. (115m)—slightly taller than the tallest tree in the world.

380 feet

...highest tree in the world?
A redwood tree in California, US. It is about 368 ft. (112m) high—over 40 times taller than the tallest person in the world.

368 feet

Who was the world's tallest person?
An American called Robert Pershing Wadlow was the world's tallest person. He was over 8 ft., 11 in. (2.7m) tall.

FACT FINDER

Find these record-breaking places in the atlas.

► The highest mountain (page 34, square J 8)

► The tallest waterfall (page 20, square E 4)

► The longest river (page 31, square L 7)

► The driest place (page 21, square E 9)

W

E

London

New York

Tokyo

What time is it?

Across the world, at the same moment, clocks show different times. This is because the world is divided into time zones. All time is measured from Greenwich, London, UK. When you cross a time zone to the east of Greenwich, time is one hour ahead. When you cross a time zone to the west of Greenwich, time is one hour behind.

The letters *am* stand for ante meridian, which means the hours from midnight until mid-day, or the morning. The letters *pm* stand for post meridian, which means the hours from mid-day until midnight, or the afternoon and evening.

If it is 12pm in London, what time is it in New York and Tokyo?

Land and sea

Imagine the world as a cake. Most of the cake would be oceans and seas, and one small slice would be the land. Most of the slice of land would be desert, rainforest, mountains, ice and grassland. Less than half the slice would be places where people can live and farm. In this atlas, you can find the biggest rainforest on page 20, see square H 5, and the biggest desert on page 30, see square E 5.

Which are the three longest rivers?

The River Nile in North Africa is 4,145 miles (6,671km) long. You could walk along its length in over four months.

The River Amazon in South America is 4,000 miles (6,437km) long. You could run along its length in over two months.

The River Yangtze in China is 3,915 miles (6,300km) long. You could cycle fast from one end to the other in just over one month.

Index

This index lists all the places on the maps in this atlas. The page number tells you which map to go to and the grid reference tells you where the place is on the map. You can find out how to look for grid references on page 9.

Abidjan p30 D10
Abu Dhabi p29 J11
Abuja p30 G9
Acapulco p18 E9
Accra p30 E10
Addis Ababa p31 N9
Adelaide p40 I9
Aden p29 F15
Afghanistan p11, p34 A7
Africa p4, p30-33, p43
Ahaggar Mountains
  p30 F5
Ahmadabad p35 E10
Al Basrah p28 G9
Al Rub al Khali
  see Empty Quarter
Alabama p17 M7
Alaska p10, p12 D4,
  p16 C3
Albania p11, p25 M7
Alberta p14 G8
Alexandria p30 L4
Algeria p10, p30 E4
Algiers p30 F2
Alice Springs p40 G5
Alma-Ata p26 G10
Alps p22 H13, p24 H5
Altai Mountains p36 F3
Altay Mountains p27 J9
Amman p28 D8
Amsterdam p22 G10
An Nafud
  see Great Sandy Desert
Anchorage p16 C4
Andaman Islands p11,
  p35 M13
Andes Mountains p21 F9
Andorra p10, p24 F6
Angola p10, p33 C11
Anguilla p10, p19 P8
Ankara p28 C5

Antananarivo p33 L12
Antarctic Circle p4, p7,
  p13 N11
Antarctica p4, p10,
  p13, p42
Antigua p10, p19 P9
Appalachian Mountains
  p17 N6
Arabian Desert p29 F12
Arabian Sea p29 J14
Aral Sea p26 E9
Archangel p26 F4
Arctic p7, p12
Arctic Circle p4, p6, p7,
  p12 C11 & G6, p14 K6,
  p16 C3, p22 B2 & H3,
  p26 E2 & O2, p27 O3
Arctic Ocean p4, p10,
  p12 E9, p14 G1, p26 G2
Argentina p10, p21 G12
Arizona p16 G8
Arkansas p17 L7
Armenia p11, p26 C9
Ashgabat p26 D11
Asia p4, p28-29, p34-39
Asmera p31 N8
Asunción p21 H10
Atacama Desert p21 E9,
  p42
Athens p25 O9
Atlantic Ocean p4, p10,
  p12 A10, p13 K5, p15
  P6, p17 P6, p19 N6,
  p21 I13, p22 A7, p24
  B3, p30 C2, p33 A10
Atlas Mountains p30 D3
Auckland p41 P9
Austin p17 K9
Australia p4, p11, p40-41
Australian Capital
  Territory p41 K9
Austria p11, p23 I12
Azerbaijan p11, p26 C9
Azores p10

Baffin Bay p12 C8
Baffin Island p12 C7,
  p15 K4

Baghdad p28 F8
Bahamas p10, p19 L7
Bahrain p11, p29 H11
Baja California p18 A3
Baku p26 C9
Bali p39 I11
Baltic Sea p23 K8
Baltimore p17 O5
Bamako p30 C8
Bandar Seri Begawan
  p38 H8
Bangalore p35 G14
Bangkok p38 D6
Bangladesh p11, p35 K10
Bangui p32 D6
Banjul p30 A8
Banks Island p14 G4
Barbados p10, p19 Q10
Barbuda p10, p19 P9
Barcelona p24 F7
Barren Desert p28 K8
Bay of Biscay p22 C12
Beijing p37 K6
Beirut p28 D7
Belarus p11, p26 C5
Belfast p22 D8
Belgium p10, p22 F10
Belgrade p25 M5
Belize p10, p18 H10
Belmopan p18 H9
Benin p10, p30 E9
Bergen p22 G6
Bering Sea p27 P2
Berlin p23 I10
Bermuda p10
Bern p22 G13
Bhutan p11, p34 K8
Bishkek p26 G10
Bissau p30 A8
Black Sea p25 Q6,
  p26 B7, p28 D4
Bogotá p20 C4
Bolivia p10, p20 F8
Bombay p35 E12
Bordeaux p22 D13
Borneo p38 H10
Bosnia-Herzegovina
  p11, p25 L5
Boston p17 P3
Botswana p10, p33 D13

Brasília p20 J7
Bratislava p23 J12
Brazil p10, p20 H6, p42
Brazzaville p32 C8
Brisbane p41 L6
British Columbia p14 E9
Brunei p11, p38 G8
Brussels p22 F10
Bucharest p25 P5
Budapest p23 K13
Buenos Aires p21 H12
Bujumbura p32 F8
Bulgaria p11, p25 O6
Burkina Faso p10,
  p30 E8
Burundi p11, p32 G8

Cabinda p10, p32 B8
Cairo p31 L4
Calcutta p35 K10
Cali p20 B5
California p16 E6, p42
Cambodia p11, p38 D7
Cameroon p10, p32 B6
Canada p10, p12 C5,
  p14-15
Canary Islands p10,
  p30 B4
Canberra p41 K9
Cape Horn p21 G17
Cape of Good Hope
  p33 D17
Cape Town p33 D16
Cape Verde Islands p10
Caracas p20 D3
Cardiff p22 D9
Caribbean p19
Caribbean Sea p19 K10,
  p20 A2
Caroline Islands p11
Casablanca p30 D2
Caspian Sea p26 C9,
  p28 H3
Cayenne p20 H3
Central African Republic
  p10, p32 C5
Central America p18-19
Chad p10, p31 I8

Chang Jiang
  see River Yangtze
Chengdu p36 I9
Cherskiy Mountains
  p27 N4
Chicago p17 M5
Chile p10, p21 E13, p42
China p11, p36 G8, p43
Chittagong p35 L10
Christchurch p41 O11
Cleveland p17 N4
Cochin p35 F15
Colombia p10, p20 C5
Colombo p35 H16
Colorado p16 H5
Colorado River p16 F7
Columbus p17 N5
Comoros p11, p33 K10
Conakry p30 B9
Congo p10, p32 C7
Connecticut p17 P3
Coober Pedy p40 H8
Copenhagen p22 I8
Coral Sea p41 K2
Corsica p11, p24 H7
Costa Rica p10, p19 J13
Crete p11, p25 P11
Croatia p11, p25 L5
Cuba p10, p19 J8
Curaçao p19 N11
Cyprus p11, p28 C7
Czech Republic p11,
  p23 J11

Dakar p30 A7
Dalian p37 L6
Dallas p17 K8
Damascus p28 D8
Dar es Salaam p32 J9
Darwin p40 G2
Dasht-E Kavir
  see Salt Desert
Dasht-E Lut
  see Barren Desert
Dead Sea p28 C8
Delaware p17 P5
Delhi p34 F8
Denmark p11, p22 H8
Denver p16 I5
Detroit p17 N4
Dhaka p34 K9

Djibouti (city) p31 O9
Djibouti (country) p11,
  p31 N8
Dodoma p32 H8
Doha p29 I11
Dominica p10, p19 Q9
Dominican Republic p10,
  p19 M8
Dubai p29 J11
Dublin p22 D8
Dubrovnik p25 M6
Dunedin p41 N13
Durban p33 G15
Dushanbe p26 F11

East China Sea p37 N8
Eastern Asia p36-37
Ecuador p10, p20 B6
Edinburgh p22 E8
Edmonton p14 G9
Egypt p11, p31 K5
El Aaiún p30 C4
El Paso p16 H8
El Salvador p10, p18 H11
Elburz Mountains p28 G7
Ellesmere Island p12 C7,
  p15 K1
Empty Quarter p29 H13
Equator p4, p6, p7, p20
  I4, p31 P12, p32 M7,
  p35 M17, p39 N6
Equatorial Guinea p10,
  p32 A7
Eritrea p11, p31 M7
Estonia p10, p23 M7
Ethiopia p11, p31 M10,
  p42
Ethiopian Highlands
  p31 N10
Europe p4, p22-26
Falkland Islands p10,
  p21 I15
Federal Republic of
  Yugoslavia p11, p25 M5

Fiji p11, p41 P4
Finland p10, p23 L4
Flores p39 K11
Florida p17 O9
Fort Worth p17 K8
France p10, p22 E12,
  p24 E4
Frankfurt p22 H11
Freetown p30 B9
French Guiana p10,
  p20 H3
Fuzhou p37 M10

Gabon p10, p32 A7
Gaborone p33 F14
Galapagos Islands p10,
  p21 A10
Gambia p10, p30 B8
Genoa p24 I5
Georgetown p20 F3
Georgia p11, p17 N7,
  p26 C8
Germany p11, p22 G10
Ghana p10, p30 D9
Gibraltar p24 B9
Gobi Desert p36 H4
Göteborg p22 I7
Great Barrier Reef p41 K3
Great Bear Lake p14 G5
Great Dividing Range
  p41 J4
Great Salt Lake p16 G5
Great Sandy Desert
  p29 E10
Great Slave Lake p14 G7
Great Victoria Desert
  p40 F8
Greater Antilles p19 J8
Greece p11, p25 N8
Greenland p10, p12 C9,
  p15 L1
Grenada p10, p19 Q11
Grenadines p10, p19 Q10
Guadeloupe p10, p19 Q9
Guam p11
Guangzhou p37 K11
Guatemala p10, p18 G10
Guatemala City p18 G10
Guinea p10, p30 B9
Guinea-Bissau p10,
  p30 A8
Gulf of Alaska p16 C6
Gulf of Mexico p17 L10,
  p18 G6
Gulf of Oman p29 K11
Gulf of St Lawrence
  p15 P10
Guyana p10, p20 F3

Hainan p37 K13
Haiti p10, p19 M9
Hanoi p38 D4
Harare p33 G12
Harbin p37 M3
Havana p19 J8
Hawaii p16 C11
Helsinki p23 L6
Himalayan
  Mountains p34 G7,
  p36 C8, p42
Hiroshima p37 O6
Ho Chi Minh City p38 E7
Hobart p41 K12
Hokkaido p37 O3

Honduras p10, p19 I10
Hong Kong p11, p37 L11
Honshu p37 P4
Houston p17 K9
Huang He
  see Yellow River
Hudson Bay p12 A7,
  p15 K8
Hungary p11, p23 K13
Hyderabad p35 G12

Ibiza p24 E9
Iceland p10, p12 C11,
  p22 B2
Idaho p16 G4
Illinois p17 L5
India p11, p35 G10, p42
Indian Ocean p11, p13
  P6, p31 P12, p33 J9,
  p35 I14, p38 B7, p40 B6
Indiana p17 M5
Indianapolis p17 M5
Indonesia p11, p38 G10
Iowa p17 K5
Iran p11, p28 J8
Iraq p11, p28 F7
Irian Jaya p11, p39 N7
Irkutsk p27 K9
Isfahan p28 I8
Islamabad p34 E6
Israel p11, p28 C8
Istanbul p25 Q7, p28 B5
Italy p11, p25 J6
Ivory Coast p10, p30 C10

Jacksonville p17 O8
Jakarta p38 G12
Jamaica p10, p19 K9
Japan p11, p37 O5

Java p38 G12
Jerusalem p28 C8
Jiddah p29 D12
Johannesburg p33 F14
Jordan p11, p28 D8

K2 (Mt Godwin
  Austen) p36 C7
Kabul p34 D6
Kalahari Desert p33 D13
Kaliningrad p23 K9,
  p26 C4
Kampala p32 H7
Kanpur p34 G9
Kansas p17 J6
Kansas City p17 K6
Kara Kum Desert
  p26 D10
Karachi p35 C10
Karakoram Range p34 E5
Kathmandu p34 I8
Kazakhstan p11, p26 E8
Kentucky p17 M6
Kenya p11, p32 I6
Khartoum p31 L8
Kiev p26 C6
Kigali p32 G7
Kingston p19 L9
Kinshasa p32 C8
Kiribati p11
Kishinev p26 B6
Kjølen Mountains p23 J4
Kolyma Mountains
  p27 O3
Kuala Lumpur p38 E9
Kuwait (city) p29 H9
Kuwait (country) p11,
  p29 F9

Kyoto p37 O6
Kyrgyzstan p11, p26 G11
Kyushu p37 O7

La Paz p20 E8
Lagos p30 F10
Lahore p34 E7
Lake Baikal p27 L8
Lake Chad p30 H8
Lake Erie p15 L13
Lake Eyre p40 H8
Lake Huron p15 L12
Lake Michigan p15 K13
Lake Nasser p31 L6
Lake Nyasa p33 H10
Lake Ontario p15 M12
Lake Superior p15 K12
Lake Tanganyika p32 G8
Lake Titicaca p20 D8
Lake Victoria p32 H7
Lake Volta p30 E10
Laos p11, p38 C5
Lapland p23 K2
Latvia p10, p11, p23 K8
Lebanon p11, p28 C8
Lesotho p10, p33 F15
Lesser Antilles p19 O10
Liberia p10, p30 B10
Libreville p32 A7
Libya p10, p30 H4
Liechtenstein p11,
  p22 H13
Lilongwe p33 H11
Lima p20 C8
Lisbon p24 A7
Lithuania p11, p23 K8
Ljubljana p25 K4
Lomé p30 E10
London p22 E10, p43
Los Angeles p16 E7
Louisiana p17 L8
Luanda p33 B9
Lusaka p33 F11
Luxembourg (city)
  p22 G11
Luxembourg (country)
  p22 G11, p11
Luzon p38 G4
Lyon p24 G4

Macao p11
Macedonia p11, p25 N7
Madagascar p11,
  p33 K12
Madeira Islands p10,
  p30 B2
Madras p35 H14
Madrid p24 C7
Magadan p27 O5

Maine p17 P2
Majorca p24 E8
Malabo p32 A6
Malawi p11, p33 H11
Malaysia p11, p38 E8
Maldive Islands p11,
  p35 E17
Mali p10, p30 D6
Malmö p23 I8
Malta p10, p25 K10
Maluku p39 K8
Managua p18 I11
Manila p38 H4
Manitoba p15 I9
Maputo p33 H14
Marrakech p30 D3
Marseille p24 G6
Marshall Islands p11
Martinique p10, p19 Q10
Maryland p17 P5
Maseru p33 F15
Mashad p28 L6
Massachusetts p17 P3
Mauritania p10, p30 B6
Mauritius p33 M13
Mayotte p11, p33 K10
Mbabane p33 G14
Mecca p29 E12
Medina p29 E11
Mediterranean Sea
  p24 F9, p28 A7, p30 F1
Melbourne p41 J10
Memphis p17 M7
Mexico p10, p18 D6
Mexico City p18 E8
Michigan p17 M4
Micronesia, States of p11
Middle East
  see South-west Asia
Milan p24 I5
Milwaukee p17 M4
Mindanao p39 J6
Minnesota p17 K2
Minorca p24 G8
Minsk p26 C5
Mississippi p17 M7
Mississippi River p17 L7
Missouri p17 L6
Missouri River p17 K5
Mogadishu p31 P11
Moldova p11, p26 B6
Monaco p11, p24 H6,
  p42
Mongolia p11, p36 H4,
  p42
Monrovia p30 B10
Montana p16 H3
Montevideo p21 I12
Montreal p15 N12
Morocco p10, p30 D3
Moscow p26 D5
Mozambique p11,
  p33 H13

Mt Aconcagua p21 F12
Mt Ararat p28 F5
Mt Elbrus p26 C8
Mt Erebus p13 N10
Mt Etna p25 K9
Mt Everest p34 J8,
  p36 D9, p42
Mt Fuji p37 P5
Mt Glittertinden p22 H5
Mt Godwin Austen *see* K2
Mt Kilimanjaro p32 H8
Mt Logan p14 D6
Mt McKinley p16 C4
Mt Olympus p25 N8
Mt Rushmore p17 I4
Mt Vesuvius p25 K8
Murmansk p26 F3
Muscat p29 L11
Myanmar p11, p38 A4

N'Djamena p30 H9
Nagasaki p37 O7
Nagpur p35 G11
Nairobi p32 I7
Namib Desert p33 B12
Namibia p10, p33 C12
Naples p25 K8
Nashville p17 M6
Nauru p11
Nebraska p17 I5
Nepal p11, p34 H8, p42
Netherlands p10, p22 G9
Nevada p16 F6
Nevis p10, p19 P9
New Brunswick p15 O11
New Caledonia p11,
  p41 N5
New Hampshire p17 P3
New Jersey p17 P4
New Mexico p16 H7
New Orleans p17 M8
New South Wales p41 K8
New York p17 O3,
  p17 P4, p43
New Zealand p11,
  p41 O12, p42
Newfoundland p15 P8
Niamey p30 E8
Nicaragua p10, p19 I11
Nicobar Islands p11,
  p35 M15
Nicosia p28 C7

Niger p10, p30 G6
Nigeria p10, p30 G10
Nizhniy Novgorod p26 E6
North America p4,
  p14-17
North Carolina p17 O6
North Dakota p17 J3
North Island p41 O8
North Korea p11, p37 M4
North Pacific Ocean
  p39 L5
North Pole p6, p12 E8
North Sea p22 F7
Northern Africa p30-31
Northern Europe p22-23
Northern Ireland p22 D8
Northern Marianas p11
Northern Territory
  p40 G4
Northwest Territories
  p14 G6
Norway p10, p12 D12,
  p22 H7
Norwegian Sea p23 J1
Nouakchott p30 A6
Nova Scotia p15 P11

Ohio p17 N5
Ohio River p17 M6
Okhotsk p27 O6
Oklahoma p17 J7
Oklahoma City p17 K7
Oman p11, p29 K13
Ontario p15 J10
Oran p30 E2
Oregon p16 E3
Oslo p22 I6
Ottawa p15 M12
Ouagadougou p30 E8

Pacific Islands p41
Pacific Ocean p10, p11,
  p13 J7, p14 A8, p16
  D11, p18 A7, p21 B12,
  p27 P13, p37 P8,
  p41 P1

Pakistan p11, p34 C8
Palau p11
Palermo p25 K9
Panama p10, p19 J13
Panama Canal p19 K12
Panama City p19 K12
Papua New Guinea p11,
  p39 O8
Paraguay p10, p21 G9
Paramaribo p20 G3
Paris p22 F11, p24 G2
Parry Islands p14 H3
Pennsylvania p17 N4
Persian Gulf p29 H10
Perth p40 C9
Peru p10, p20 C7
Philadelphia p17 P4
Philippines p11, p38 H5
Phnom Penh p38 E7
Phoenix p16 G7
Poland p11, p23 K10
Pontine Mountains
  p28 E5
Port Moresby p39 P8
Port-au-Prince p19 M9
Porto p24 B6
Porto-Novo p30 E10
Portugal p10, p24 A6
Prague p23 I11
Pretoria p33 F14
Prince Edward Island
  p15 P11
Prince of Wales
  Island p15 I4
Príncipe p10, p30 F12
Puerto Rico p10, p19 O9
Pyongyang p37 M5
Pyrenees p24 D6

Qatar p11, p29 I11
Qingdao p37 L6
Quebec p15 N9
Queen Elizabeth
  Islands p15 J2
Queensland p41 I5
Quetta p34 C8
Quito p20 B5

Rabat p30 D2
Recife p20 M5
Red Sea p29 C10,
  p31 M5
Republic of Ireland p10,
  p22 B8
Republic of South
  Africa p10, p33 D14
Réunion p33 M13
Reykjavík p22 B3
Rhode Island p17 P3

Riga p23 L8
Rio de Janeiro p20 K9
Rio Grande p16 I8,
  p18 E4
River Amazon p20 F5,
  p43
River Amu Darya p26 E11
River Amur p27 O8
River Brahmaputra
  p34 K8
River Danube p23 I12,
  p25 O5
River Darling p41 K7
River Don p26 D7
River Elbe p22 H9
River Euphrates p28 E6
River Ganges p35 H9
River Godavari p35 G11
River Helmand p34 B7
River Indus p34 D8
River Irrawaddy P38 B5
River Irtysh p26 H9
River Kasai p32 C8
River Lena p27 L5
River Loire p22 D12,
  p24 F3
River Mackenzie p14 F5
River Mekong p38 D5
River Murray p41 I9
River Narmada p35 E10
River Nelson p15 J9
River Niger p30 F9
River Nile p31 L7, p43
River Ob p26 H6
River Orange p33 C15
River Orinoco p20 D3
River Paraná p21 H11
River Po p25 J5
River Rhine p22 G11
River Rhône p22 F13,
  p24 G5
River São Francisco
  p20 K7
River Seine p22 F12,
  p24 G3
River St Lawrence
  p15 N11
River Tagus p24 C7
River Tigris p28 F7
River Volga p26 D7
River Yangtze p37 I9, p43
River Yenisey p27 J6
River Yukon p14 E5
River Zaire p32 E7
River Zambezi p33 E11
Riyadh p29 G11
Rocky Mountains p14 E6,
  p16 G3
Romania p11, p25 N4
Rome p25 J7
Ronne Ice Shelf p13 L7
Ross Ice Shelf p13 M9
Ross Sea p13 M10

Rotorua p41 P9
Russia p11, p12 H8,
  p26 G7, p27, p42
Rwanda p11, p32 F7
Ryukyu Islands p11,
  p37 O8

Sahara Desert p30 E5
Sakhalin Island p27 P7
Salt Desert p28 J7
San Antonio p17 K9
San Diego p16 F7
San Francisco p16 E6
San Jose p16 E16
San José p19 J12
San Juan p19 O9
San Marino p11, p25 J6
San Salvador p18 H11
Sana p29 F14
Santiago p21 F12
Santo Domingo p19 N9
São Paulo p21 K9
São Tomé p10, p30 F11
Sapporo p37 P3
Sarajevo p25 M6
Sardinia p11, p24 H8
Saskatchewan p14 G9
Saudi Arabia p11,
  p29 F12
Sea of Japan p37 O3
Sea of Okhotsk p27 O6
Seattle p16 E2
Senegal p10, p30 A7
Seoul p37 N6
Serbia see Federal
  Republic of Yugoslavia

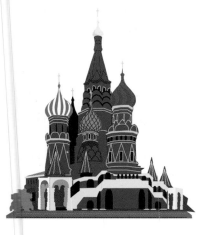

Seville p24 B8
Seychelles p11, p32 L8
Shanghai p37 M8
Shenyang p37 M5
Shikoku p37 O6
Siberia p27 M7
Sicily p11, p25 K9
Sierra Leone p10, p30 B9
Sierra Madre p18 C4
Singapore p11, p38 F9
Skopje p25 N7
Slovakia p11, p23 K12
Slovenia p11, p25 K5
Socotra p11, p29 J16
Sofia p25 N6
Solomon Islands p11,
 p41 N2
Somalia p11, p31 P9
South America p4, p9,
 p20-21, p43
South Australia p40 G7
South Carolina p17 O7
South China Sea
 p37 M12, p38 E3
South Dakota p17 I4
South Georgia p10
South Island p41 M11
South Korea p11, p37 M6
South Pole p6, p13 M8
South-east Asia p38-39
South-west Asia p28-29
Southern Africa p32-33
Southern Alps p41 N12
Southern Asia p34-35
Southern Europe p24-25
Spain p10, p24 C8
Sri Lanka p11, p35 I15
St Kitts p10, p19 P9
St Louis p17 I6
St Lucia p10, p19 Q10
St Petersburg p26 D4
St Vincent p10, p19 Q10
Stockholm p23 J7
Sudan p11, p31 K8
Suez Canal p31 M4
Sulawesi p39 J9
Sumatra p38 E10
Sumba p39 J11

Surinam p10, p20 G3
Svalbard Islands p12 E10
Swaziland p11, p33 G14
Sweden p10, p11,
 p12 D12, p23 J5
Switzerland p11, p22 G13
Sydney p41 L8
Syria p11, p28 D7

Tabriz p28 G6
Taipei p37 M10
Taiwan p11, p37 M10
Tajikistan p11, p26 G11
Takla Makan Desert
 p36 D6
Tallinn p23 L6
Tanami Desert p40 G5
Tanzania p11, p33 H9
Tashkent p26 F10
Tasmania p11, p41 J11
Taurus Mountains p28 C6
Tbilisi p26 C8
Tegucigalpa p18 H11
Tehran p28 I7
Tel Aviv p28 C8
Tennessee p17 M7
Texas p17 J9
Thailand p11, p38 C5
Thar Desert p34 D8
Thimpu p34 K8
Tianjin p37 K6
Tibet p36 E7
Tien Shan Mountains
 p36 D4
Tierra del Fuego p21 H16
Timor p39 K11
Tiranë p25 M7
Tobago p10, p19 Q11
Togo p10, p30 E9
Tokyo p37 P5, p43
Tonga p41 Q5
Toronto p15 M12
Trinidad p10, p19 Q11
Tripoli p30 H3
Trondheim p22 I4
Tropic of Cancer p6, p7,
 p17 L11, p19 N7,
 p29 A11, p30 A5,
 p32 I1, p35 A10,
 p37 Q9, p38 D3
Tropic of Capricorn p6,
 p7, p21 D10, p33 A13,
 p39 Q13, p40 B6
Tunis p30 H2
Tunisia p10, p30 G3
Turin p24 H5
Turkey p11, p25 P7,
 p28 D5
Turkmenistan p11,
 p26 E11
Tuvalu p11, p41 P3

Uganda p11, p32 G6
Ukraine p11, p26 C6
Ulan Bator p36 I3
United Arab Emirates p11,
 p29 I11
United Kingdom p10,
 p22 E8
United States p10,
 p16-17, p42
Ural Mountains p26 F7
Uruguay p10, p21 I11
Utah p16 G6
Uzbekistan p11, p26 E10

Vancouver p14 E10
Vanuatu p11, p41 N3
Vatican City p11,
 p25 J7, p42
Venezuela p10,
 p20 D3, p42
Venice p25 J5
Verkhoyausk
 Mountains p27 M5
Vermont p17 P3
Victoria Island p12 C6,
 p14 H5
Victoria p41 J10
Vienna p23 J12
Vientiane p38 D5
Vietnam p11, p38 E5
Vilnius p23 L9
Vinhdaya Range p35 F10
Virgin Islands p10,
 p19 P9
Virginia p17 O5
Vishakhapatnam p35 I12
Vladivostok p27 O10
Volgograd p26 D7

Warsaw p23 K10
Washington p16 E2
Washington DC p17 O5
Weddell Sea p13 K6
Wellington p41 P10
West Virginia p17 O5
Western Australia p40 D8
Western Sahara p10,
 p30 B5
Western Samoa p41 Q3
Windhoek p33 C13
Winnipeg p15 J11
Wisconsin p17 L4
Wyoming p16 H4

Xian p37 J8

Yablonovyy
 Mountains p27 I8
Yangon p38 B6
Yaoundé p32 B6
Yellow River p37 K7
Yellow Sea p37 M7
Yemen p11, p29 H14
Yerevan p26 C9
Yukon River p16 C3
Yukon Territory p14 E5

Zagreb p25 L4
Zagros Mountains
 p28 H7
Zaire p10, p32 E8
Zambia p10, p33 E11
Zanzibar Island p32 J8
Zimbabwe p11, p33 F12